The 48 – a tribute to the men of Surrey CCC in the First World War

2018

Written by
Philip Paine with Daniel Norcross

Designed by
Dan Johnstone
Glaucia Orlandin

© Surrey CCC 2018.

ISBN: 978-1-909811-43-0

Contents

Editor's note	7
Special Acknowledgements	12
Introduction	14
The War Memorial	22
Places of Birth	24
Schools Attended	26
Ranks at Death	28
Place of Burial or Memorial	30
Chronological Order of Deaths	32
Charles Pelham Gardner Aldrich	34
Ernest Attwater	38
Henry George Blacklidge	42
William Matthew Burrell	46
Hubert Pennington Cattley	50
Esme Fairfax Chinnery	52
Harry Broderick Chinnery	60
George Stanley Cooper	66
Wilfred John Hutton Curwen	70
Wilfred Leedham Dawson	78
Hugh Murray Forster	80
William Gerald Oliver Gill	84
Francis Sydney Gillespie	90
Reginald Nigel Gipps	94
C Green	98
Arthur Kendrick Hickman	102
Charles Morgan Hoare	108
Bernard Henry Holloway	112
John Howell	116
Frank Lewis Hunt	122
John Henry Sneyd Hunt	126
Dudley Mark Hayward Jewell	132
Albert William Lane-Joynt	138

Richard Percy Lewis	142
Edward Longton	146
Alan Marshal	148
Harold Gostwyck May	152
Edwin Bertram Myers	160
John William Washington Nason	166
Frank Leslie Nightingale	172
Harold Thomas Noakes	176
Erasmus Darwin Parker	182
Howard Roderick Parkes	186
John Edward Raphael	190
Arthur Beddome Read	198
Wilfred Francis Reay	202
Francis Watson Robarts	204
Elvin Alfred Scott MC	208
Victor George Fleetwood Shrapnel	210
Charles Caldwell Sills	214
Christopher Snell	218
Thomas Colegrave Stafford	222
Arthur Burrell Thorne	226
Carleton Wyndham Tufnell	230
Horatio Spencer Walpole	234
Walter Victor Patrick Charles Whittle	240
Guy Wormald	244
Philip Cecil Wynter	248
Surrey Yearbooks	252
Appendix 1 – John Raphael's	
Travel Journal	256
Appendix 2 – Arthur Hickman's Letters	
from the Front	262
Appendix 3 – A New View of The Oval	266
Acknowledgements	268

The historian Edmond Taylor in his book *The Fossil Monarchies* wrote: "The First World War killed fewer victims than the Second World War, destroyed fewer buildings, and uprooted millions instead of tens of millions - but in many ways it left even deeper scars both on the mind and on the map of Europe. The old world never recovered from the shock." The world that the 48 men featured in this book inhabited was very much that old world; the world before the tragically ill-named "war to end all wars".

For the majority of these men it was a world framed by public school attendance, personal affluence, membership of Gentlemen's Clubs and a shared love of cricket, that game whose very name evokes even now chivalric values and an aesthetic that is as antithetical to the horrors of the Great War as it is possible to imagine. The Germans and English were not playing football with each other on a daily basis between bouts of half-hearted sniper fire. The Great War was the first mechanised global conflict. Tanks superseded horse-backed cavalry. Bombs were, for the first time, dropped from the air. Chemical weapons were liberally used by both sides. Killing was perpetrated on an industrial scale. It is estimated that around 10 million military personnel lost their lives in these four years. It

was into this rapidly changing, brutal and unique environment that the 48 men commemorated on the Surrey CCC war memorial were hurled, never to return.

This book, commissioned by Surrey CCC, cannot hope to explain why the war happened, or chart the massive socio-economic changes that took place during its four years. It doesn't seek to give a narrative of the war or a synopsis of the military tactics in the many and varied theatres in which armed struggle took place. Nor can it hope adequately to provide a comprehensive account of each of the men's lives featured briefly within its pages. It is purely and simply a means of remembering that behind the names written on a rather spartan wooden tablet hung in the pavilion at The Oval are lives of mostly young men, connected to each other through their involvement with Surrey CCC and their deaths in the Great War.

The author of this book, Philip Paine, was initially motivated by his interest in identifying the graves of, and memorials to, cricketers who lost their lives in the war. But this book has morphed into something slightly more complex. Most of the men featured never played first-class cricket. Although a fair number did turn out for minor representative teams, the vast bulk are "ordinary" men. Few details remain of their brief lives. So this is not a book about cricketers per se. But what Philip's lengthy and painstaking research has unearthed is a profile of 48 lives that provides a window into that old world to which Edmond Taylor alluded.

There are naturally frustrations that abound for anyone tasked with editing such a project. Up until very near the deadline for submission to the publisher, the man about whom we knew the least was Charles Aldrich, the first man on the memorial board. I was even tempted at one point to depart from an alphabetical listing of the casualties so as to put the more in-depth biographies at the front to maintain the reader's attention, but this would have been to confer a weight on the lives of some men over others; and that is not what this book is about.

Furthermore, with the centenary of the outbreak of war there came a large number of new initiatives around the world that made details available about Great War casualties that simply weren't there when Philip began his research. Deciding when to stop collecting information has therefore been a challenge. How much should we include about their military careers? How much about their school lives? How far back should we take the family tree? In the end we took decisions on a case-by-case basis. Some of the men such as Alan Marshal and John Raphael had good first-class cricketing careers so we focused mainly on that aspect of their lives. For others, many of whom left school, enlisted and were dead within months of arriving at the front, the circumstances of their deaths and whatever we could glean from their school files have formed the vast bulk of their biographies. But for some, such as Wilfred Dawson and Edward Longton, there simply was very little out there to be found. But then why would there be? The 48 men in this book are connected solely through their interest in Surrey

CCC. They are not in and of themselves people about whom one may choose to write a book. They had, like most people, unremarkable lives. It is through their remarkable deaths that they have been brought together.

For my own part it has been a fascinating and illuminating experience. Thoughtlessly perhaps, it had never occurred to me before that the school and university one attends affords privileges not just in life, but also in death. Philip was able to establish the schools that thirty-four of the casualties attended. Of these, all but two were public schools. For these men we have tended to find far more information than for the other sixteen. Oxbridge colleges have also kept marvellous records in most cases, including team photographs, as well as information on academic performance and military careers. Dulwich College, for example, has maintained extraordinarily detailed reports on its four former pupils featured in this book which has been at once hugely gratifying to me and also, as an alumnus of that institution, something of a concern. I'm pretty sure I don't want anyone looking at my file!

The biggest challenge Philip faced was in making the book more than simply a collection of facts about birth, parents, school attended and death, accompanied by a photograph of the casualty and/or his grave. And it is in the smaller details that Philip has done most justice to his subjects. We discover for example that John Nason had a hastily convened wedding witnessed only by his mother-in-law and sister-in-law, much to the horror no doubt of his own parents, and that Wilfred Curwen gave his address as The Bath Club on which PG Wodehouse based his fictional Drones Club. There are the terribly poignant details such as the letter that William Gill's father wrote to his school apologising for not having done it sooner by saying: "The fact is I shirk diving into matters connected with our dear boy who is gone & opening up wounds which, though I am not morbid, probably never will be far below the surface. Gerald [William's middle name] was a singular mixture. Very keen on Sports & painstaking to excel in them, yet with a disposition more like a lovable girl's than a sporting youth's." Or the fact that Carleton Tufnell played a match in which eight participants that day were to die in the war.

There are some who met shocking deaths, such as George Cooper, who was killed by two of his own troops. His murder was reported in that wonderfully evocative contemporary idiom and included the observation that "the two murderers are reported to have been of a morose and fanatical disposition." Such elegance of language combined with quite startling understatements abound, especially in the tributes of Commanding Officers. Describing the events that led up to Harry Chinnery's death, his CO commented: "It was a trying night, and he did splendidly all the earlier part of it in keeping them at their work and keeping up their spirits." The letter that Harold May sent from what was to be his deathbed is a masterpiece in maintaining a stiff upper lip. In recounting the injury he received which was ultimately to kill him two weeks later he wrote: "One shell burst alongside me and sent me toppling down the hill into a pond at the bottom. It felt just like being popped on the thigh at the footer, though of course the shell made a beastly mess of the leg."

With the casualties listed alphabetically, the reader will also spot some remarkable coincidences. Dudley Jewell and Albert Lane-Joynt, who appear next to each other in this book, are buried in the same cemetery and died four weeks apart. Harold Noakes, the youngest of the 48 to die, aged 18, comes immediately before the wonderfully named Erasmus Darwin Parker who, at 48, is the oldest. And coincidences with my own life have flown out of the pages at me. Alan Marshal died in the hospital, Imtarfa in Malta, where

my grandfather was treated for wounds after being on active service in the same Gallipoli campaign. Elvin Scott was born on the same road as my brother, Nightingale Lane, and Frank Nightingale lived on the same road as my first girlfriend. The names of streets I have visited and driven down crop up frequently. Naturally there is a pretty decent chance of that happening if you have lived your entire life in south west London and are editing a book on people with connections to Surrey CCC but for many readers there will be similar curiosities.

There is also for the cricket fanatic an inescapable sense of waste. John Howell, who was just 20 when he died, was thought of at Repton well into the 1950s as the best player that school had ever produced; better even than the great CB Fry. Albert Lane-Joynt, another who would not reach his twenty-first birthday, was described in an article in the *Cricketer* as the finest young cricket writer of his generation. But these men excelled not just at cricket. Carleton Tufnell, 22 when he died, was a prodigious all-round sportsman at Eton, and Victor Shrapnel, as well as taking 197 wickets at an average of 6.75 while at Wilson's Grammar School, also broke the long-jump record and the mile record, captained the chess team, the debating society and achieved a place at Magdalen College, Oxford when just 17 years old.

The reader will also notice how incredibly wealthy many of the casualties were on their death. We debated whether to include probate details (where we have them), but in the end decided they help to illustrate the world from which these men came. When the 23-year-old Reginald Gipps died he left an estate valued at just short of £78,000. There is no wholly accurate way of converting this figure to modern money but as a general rule of thumb inflation has increased the value of a pound by around 64 times over the last 100 years. This does not take into account the hyper-inflation in the housing market. If one were to calculate it by that measure alone you would end up with a figure of nearer 200 times. So Gipps' fortune at such a young age was worth around £5 million today (or £15 million if he had sunk it into property).

For me, though, the value in showing these figures comes out more in the anomalies, the biggest of whom perhaps is Hubert Pennington Cattley. Cattley remains a frustratingly enigmatic figure about whom we could glean very few facts, but the ones we have hint at a rather extraordinary man. Educated at Eton and later Merton College, Oxford from where he failed to complete his degree, he is one of only two Privates among the 48, the other being the Australian cricketer Alan Marshal. This is in itself most curious. Every other man in this book who attended public school and/or Oxbridge was swiftly promoted to 2nd Lieutenant or above. Cattley fought for two years but was never promoted. His family contained Liberal MPs and radical suffragettes, and had houses in central London and very likely large fortunes, yet at his death Cattley left a mere £154 – 18s – 9d. Philip got close to tracking down more information from a distant relative, but the trail went cold, so the reader is left to imagine what may have caused a man from such a privileged background, at a time when this mattered perhaps more than ever, to drop out of university and become a bank clerk before dying a Private aged 26.

As for the illustrations, Philip has done a remarkable job in finding either a photograph of nearly every casualty and/or a picture of his grave or memorial. The first book I ever cherished, read and re-read until it fell apart, was David Frith's *England v Australia: a Pictorial History*. I was eight years old and with this book I plighted my troth to cricket for a lifetime. Without doubt it was the pre-1914 illustrations that intoxicated me the most. Was it because I was looking back into that old world that Edmond Taylor had identified? To gaze into the eyes of many

of these young men is often to see people who have aged way before their time; men who have transitioned from the old world of their childhood to a new world of unimaginable horrors. Albert Lane-Joynt and Charles Sills could both easily pass for men twice their age. But in contrast the jaunty Reginald Gipps, smiling vivaciously into a camera without a care in the world, is perhaps just as poignant, as is Ernest Attwater sporting a cheeky grin in a team photo taken just four days before war was declared.

Ultimately this book is about honouring these 48 men by remembering them as people; often humble, unremarkable people who would never have expected to be, or even wanted to be, subjects of a book written some 100 years after their deaths. These men are emblematic of all the men whose names appear on memorials across the world. And whilst it may be impossible to escape a certain sense of morbidity whilst pondering lives cut short, often senselessly and always tragically, I do hope that the reader will identify in these brief biographies something more nuanced than just the massive scale this cataclysm wrought on nations worldwide, for nations are nothing if they are not the people in those nations. People who frequently have "History" inflicted upon them. Our understanding of past events is too often seen through the prism of the supposedly "big picture" in which the major actors are Kings and Presidents, Generals and politicians. If you let yourself look, sometimes the simple image of a careworn Charles Sills or a carefree Ernest Attwater can tell you much more.

Daniel Norcross

•••••••••••••••••••••••••••••••••••••••

On subsequent pages I have listed those people whose assistance helped to bring this book to fruition. Each one supplied a worthwhile piece of information or a photograph which I would not have found myself and they allowed me to illustrate a part of the life of a casualty much more thoroughly.

I would however like to put on record a special note of thanks to Sussex CCC member, eminent cricket and local historian and author Roger Packham. He is currently researching Sussex CCC cricketers who were killed in action and suggested that I do some research on those listed on the war memorial at The Oval. Little did I realise when I began how many people this would bring me into contact with and where my travels to get this information would take me. It has been an enjoyable two years of research, made considerably easier by help from the Internet.

More thanks must go to Jo Miller, librarian at Surrey CCC, for help during the many hours I spent doing research in the library, the many members of the excellent Great War Forum website who answered my requests for help about the military careers of many in this book, but who answered under aliases and whose identity I do not know, and Surrey CCC who allowed me to use the photographs of the war memorial and 1911 players and members painting.

Though far from exhaustively, I would like to thank John Surtees, Communications Manager at Surrey CCC, without whose encouragement and willingness to commission this book I may never have got it completed. And thanks also to Daniel Norcross for removing most of my extraneous semi-colons, and being prepared to include numerous additions to the manuscript right up to the publishing deadline.

••

The great Jack Hobbs, Surrey and England's most popular cricketer before and after the Great War.

Like so many others, whilst ambling aimlessly around the Long Room at Kennington Oval cricket ground, I have looked up at the wooden memorial that commemorates 48 people killed in the 1914-18 war and read through the names.

I will get my minor moans about the memorial out of the way right now, which are: 1) that the initials MC which stand for Military Cross are etched too close to the initials of EA Scott, so are easily missed; 2) that AB Thorne's name has a puncture mark on the "B" which could do with a repair; 3) that Walpole's name is out of sequence and in the wrong column; 4) that some show their Christian names, eg John Howell, Alan Marshal and Guy Wormald, whereas the rest have just their initials shown and; 5) that some of the ranks attained by the deceased are omitted and some differ when compared to the records held by the Commonwealth War Graves Commission (CWGC).

Now that my moans are complete I am very pleased that the club saw fit to get this memorial erected for those who fell in the Great War and that it is situated in an area frequented by so many on match days; especially when the rain has set in.

There is a second war memorial in the Long Room at the other end, and it is tidily engraved with the words: "In memory of the members, players and staff of the Surrey CCC who lost their lives in the Second World War 1939-45." Alas it has no names engraved on it.

I should explain that I have written this book from the perspective of why these names are on this memorial. I am no military historian, and feel unable to write about their respective military careers. If I had decided to research the lives and careers of 48 individuals who served in different battalions and regiments and in different theatres of war, it would have been extremely arduous and time-consuming. I would also have risked omitting some important facts about their careers and caused offence. I did however seek advice from some military websites which led to a lot of information being sent to me about some individuals, so I have included these details. Information passed to me by their respective schools often contained details about their military life, so I have also woven this into my own cricket research.

I make mention of De Ruvigny's throughout the book. The 9th Marquis of Ruvigny and Raineval compiled five volumes containing

26,000 biographies of men who fought in the army, navy and air-force and who died during the Great War. Of these about 7,000 contain photographs and if not, then many give a good write-up on parents, school, early years, details of regiment, promotions, interests and date and place of death. Although the volumes cover the length of the war, most included died in its opening years. It was a commercially produced series published in the 1920s and is today referred to as De Ruvigny's. This is one key reason among many others why the level of detail I have been able to establish about the 48 will differ greatly and may not fully reflect each of their lavish careers.

Thirteen of those listed on the Surrey war memorial attained the rank of Captain and many went to top-rate public schools. If an ability to play cricket is also factored in, then some of these Commissioned Officers would probably be worthy of a lengthy biography in their own right, so condensing their achievements into a couple of pages feels like an insult. Similarly the lives and careers of Marshal, Nightingale and Raphael could easily justify whole books to themselves owing to their cricketing achievements.

Of the three forces, the Army features most prominently, but one must not forget the heroics and losses inflicted on the Royal Flying Corps (which later became the Royal Air Force); the average lifespan of a pilot was just 18 hours "in the air". Jack Hobbs, who was the subject of considerable opprobrium in the early years of the war for his initial failure to enlist, eventually joined the Royal Flying Corps. Four of his five brothers fought in the war and two were badly wounded.

There is no one alive who knew any of the 48 casualties, fought with or played cricket with them, so except where I have been able to unearth any mentions of their personalities or traits, these will unfortunately remain unknown. Therefore the book will be lacking in breadth

from that perspective and the write-ups will at times be a little two-dimensional and impersonal.

I have endeavoured to write at least a page on each casualty and add a photograph that relates to their life or death. In some instances it will be of them, in other instances it will be of their grave or a memorial on which they are listed. There are some delightful and now unfamiliar middle names for some of these casualties which can easily be explained; in this era as well as it being popular for the son's middle name to be his father's first name, it was also popular for the maiden name of his mother to be included.

The much hallowed and loved "Golden Age" of cricket came to an end following the declaration of war on August 4th 1914. Although this era is often seen through rose-tinted glasses, Nottinghamshire, Somerset and Worcestershire were in financial trouble and feared for their respective futures. There were no Test matches that summer and when war was declared crowds at county matches began to dwindle. Many trains were requisitioned by the War Office and perhaps interest just faded as grey clouds gathered over Europe.

Surrey "won" the title in 1914, although perhaps "won" should not be the word used to describe their achievement. Come September Surrey were top of the County Championship, but the last two rounds of matches were called off so they were considered County Champions. They were six points clear of Kent in third place, but had played eight matches more than Middlesex in second place. However these were the days of the title being decided by the acquisition of percentage of possible points and as Surrey had 74%, they were ahead of Middlesex (70%) and Kent (62.143%). Of their 28 matches, they had won 15, drawn eight, lost two, seen two abandoned and had one that was not to be counted in the totting up of points.

Jack Hobbs scored 11 centuries during the season and was the first batsman to reach 2,000 runs. It was also his benefit season, but his benefit match against Kent had to be played at Lord's after The Oval, like so many trains, and, ultimately, so many lives, had been requisitioned by the War Office.

Both The Oval and Lord's hosted representative matches throughout the Great War and many of these are reported in the war-time yearbooks for Surrey CCC. The Lancashire and Yorkshire leagues however, continued throughout the period. Jack Hobbs played for Idle CC, Idle being a suburb of Bradford. His Surrey team-mate Bill Hitch played for Eccleshill. The legendary SF Barnes played for Saltaire, Fred Root for Bowling Old Lane, and Jack Hearne, Frank Woolley and Schofield Haigh all played for Keighley.

210 professional first-class cricketers enlisted to fight, along with many more players. These were, after all, the days of amateur and professional and of course many who played for the Universities died too. Surrey's Ernie Hayes, Bill Hitch and Andy Sandham joined The Sportsman's Battalion of the Royal Fusiliers. Neville Knox joined the Public School's Battalion, whilst Herbert Strudwick and William Smith worked in munitions in South London.

On December 11th 1914 *The Times* published a list of players who were serving in the armed forces. The Surrey cricketers on the list were: "CTA Wilkinson, DJ Knight, J Howell, MC Bird, PGH Fender, HD Leveson-Gower, M Freeman, Attwater, Bungay, Ernie Hayes, Bill (JW) Hitch, Andrew Sandham, Alan Peach, Edwin Myers, Lord Dalmeny, RH Lagden, JP Raphael and EM Dowson." The inconsistency of use of first names and initials apparently infected *The Times* just as badly as it did the Surrey war memorial itself!

Approximately three-quarters of registered first-class cricketers went on to serve in the Great

War and when it ended over four years later, 290 of them were dead. The "winding down" of cricket was not consistent across the globe. In South Africa there was no cricket played after the MCC tour of 1913/14. Australia wound up their cricket on July 10th 1915. New Zealand meanwhile played right through the 1915 season and India carried on regardless. In the West Indies however it ceased as soon as war was declared.

After hostilities had ended cricket began again in New Zealand on Christmas Day 1918, in Australia on Boxing Day, in England during the spring of 1919 when the country experimented with two-day matches, in South Africa in 1919 and in West Indies in 1920.

Yorkshire CCC recently unveiled a memorial at Headingley to their players who were killed in action in both world wars, but there are only five names listed on it. In the summer of 2014 Sussex CCC also unveiled a memorial to their players and staff that died in both wars. Nine are listed for the Great War and two for the 1939-45 war. The first-class counties suffered varying numbers of casualties. Of the 290 first-class cricketers who were killed in the Great War, the two Universities suffered the worst with Cambridge contributing 23 war dead and Oxford 36. Of the 17 counties, Hampshire had the most fatalities with a remarkable 24.

Yet the memorial in the pavilion at The Oval lists 48 and it relates only to the First World War. That one county apparently lost over nine times more than another intrigued me, yet the reason for this will become clear.

Despite my interest in the history of Surrey CCC, most of the names on the memorial were unfamiliar to me. My first avenue of research was the CWGC website which lists most of the Commonwealth casualties in both wars. The website also gives their rank, any gallantry medals awarded to them, place of burial and often next-of-kin details as well as their address. As expected, there was a big variety of ranks, from Private to Lieutenant Colonel and deaths occurred in each year of the war. Although most casualties were killed in Belgium and France, some died in Greece, India, Iraq, Israel and Malta. Regrettably, some are listed on large memorials to those with no known grave, as their bodies were either never found, or were found with no identification on them and so interred under a cream CWGC headstone, engraved with only "Known Unto God."

Armed with these details I then checked the ever-expanding and very detailed Cricketarchive website and established that only eight – Blacklidge, both Chinnerys, Curwen, Gillespie, Marshal, Myers and Raphael – played first-class cricket for Surrey CCC. However, Lewis played first-class matches for Middlesex and non first-class for Surrey. Nason appeared in first-class matches for Cambridge University, Gloucestershire and Sussex, Parkes in first-class matches for Warwickshire and London County, and Holloway first-class for Sussex. So who are the others and why are they listed on the memorial?

I then turned my attention to the Surrey CCC annual yearbooks between 1890 and 1914 which in this period listed the members of the club and showed results of matches involving the second XI, Gentlemen of Surrey, Surrey Young Amateurs XI and Surrey Club and Ground. I checked each yearbook for any mentions of the 48 casualties being members of the club and then again for any evidence of them playing for the club. I was then able to connect many more names on the memorial to the club. I hope that I have not missed any appearances for lesser Surrey teams in my quest to highlight as many teams as possible that were represented, but appearances for first XIs and in first-class

matches will be accurate as they are easy to find.

Further success came when I checked the schoolboy member section and found the names of Gipps, Hickman, Howell, Longton, Noakes and Scott. Likewise when I checked the committee details listed on the first few pages I found that J.H. Hunt had been on the Finance Committee in 1914.

The committee meeting minutes for May 6th 1915 held at the Surrey Historical Centre in Woking (page 219, minute number 22) tell that "Each amateur was awarded a silver cigarette box inscribed with the autographs of the players, for winning the championship in 1914." Myers is the only casualty to have played this season, but he was a professional.

The same volume of minutes refers to a meeting on February 18th 1915 (page 211) when the topic is football: "Crystal Palace FC asked to play the remainder of their matches at The Oval – not entertained."

On August 17th 1916 (page 256, minute number 4) the minutes show that "the Acting Hon Secretary reported that the number of members paid for 1916, 2,100 as against 2,584 at corresponding meeting in 1915. Abroad 286." According to a club yearbook, as many as 1,905 members paid in 1917 and this despite the obvious fact that county cricket was not being played at the ground during the war. Many members answered the club's call for help and continued to pay their annual subscriptions.

The committee meeting minutes contain a wealth of extra information which shows how the war was affecting the club. The minutes for a meeting on November 15th 1917 (page 287, minute number 2) report that the Royal Flying Corps was using the west wing of the pavilion for sleeping and living purposes.

On page 89 of the 1919 yearbook it says: "The loss of service of EF Chinnery, HB Chinnery, WJH Curwen, FS Gillespie, John Howell, JH Hunt, RP Lewis, FL Nightingale, JE Raphael, FW Robarts, E Attwater, HG Blacklidge, A Marshal, EB Myers and WH Smith, valuable members past and present of the first XI, second XI, Committee and Staff is deplored." It is interesting to note that the names are not listed in alphabetical order and that Howell's first name is used, as it is on the memorial. The last name, WH Smith is not listed on the memorial and all attempts to trace him via the CWGC web-site and Surrey CCC yearbooks have proved futile, due to his surname being so common. I found seven WH Smith's whose last known address or parents' address was in Surrey, or close to The Oval, but this led to nothing conclusive. Was he a Surrey CCC member? In the yearbooks between 1912 and 1914 is a member listed as Lieut.-Col. W Haskett Smith although tracing his death has not been possible. This WH Smith is not listed on the memorial, perhaps news of his death was incorrect and he survived the war.

It would be intriguing to know if any of the casualties fought together, or which ones met any others. Sadly without battalion diaries and the make-up of the relevant regiments it has not been possible to establish one way or the other. However, John Hunt and Edwin Myers, who were both killed in the Somme area, were both in the London Regiment and killed on successive days, so it is highly likely that they were fighting very close to each other. Likewise Harold Noakes and John Raphael both went to Merchant Taylor's School in North London, albeit about a decade apart. Both died within six weeks of each other and are buried in a huge cemetery just a few yards apart.

Thirty of those listed on the memorial were Surrey CCC members and some played first-class matches for the club or for the second XI, Gentlemen of Surrey or lesser teams, but some did not play any cricket. Thus it is clear to see that names are listed on the memorial for a variety of connections with the club.

In the Committee minutes for November 20th 1919 under the title "War Memorial" is the following: "It was decided that a War memorial to those who fell in the War should be provided, to include Amateur and Professional players of the first and second XIs, whether Members of the Club or not, Members of the Staff and Members of the Club, and that it be referred to the Ground Committee to report on appropriate form of memorial, estimate cost and where it shall be placed."

If we ignore those who played for the first and second XIs, we are left with 11 names to account for. Of these 11, Attwater, Gill, Jewell, May, Sills and Thorne all played for the Young Amateurs. Clearly this was enough to get them included on the war memorial. So we are left with five to account for. Reay played for Gentlemen of Surrey and Green is unknown, so only Shrapnel, Snell and Walpole's relationships with the club cannot be established, although the latter, along with hundreds of others, did play for the Club and Ground XI. As he was related to the famous Walpole family my speculation is that he was employed by the club in some capacity, or perhaps was a benefactor.

I had expected schoolboy members not to progress to full membership until aged 21, but this does not seem to be the case, as some, like Hickman and Hoare were full members when aged 19 and Lane-Joynt even younger.

On page 73 of the 1922 Surrey CCC yearbook, amongst the annual report, there is an amendment to Rule 1: "The Surrey County Cricket Club, hereinafter called the Club, shall consist of not more than 5,000 members of whom not more than 4,150, hereinafter called Full Members, shall be Gentlemen and not more than 400 shall be School-boy Members. The remainder, not exceeding in aggregate 450, shall consist of Lady Members and School-girl Members. No person under the age of 14 years shall be eligible as a member." Some of those listed on the war memorial were still "School-boy" members, which encompassed cricket lovers who were aged below 21. The age at which one could become a member before this rule change has not been established.

I checked the *Wisden Almanacks* that cover the war years and a couple of editions post-war. They are understandably sparser than most editions, but contain a distressingly large collection of obituaries for the first-class and schoolboy cricketers who were cut down in their prime. These often very brief obituaries regularly mention which school the casualty attended, so I then contacted these mainly public schools. Most replied to my emails and their respective archive departments sent me some excellent documents which have added much to my own research. As well as details about their schooldays, information about their military career, their obituary in the school magazine and a photograph were often hastily despatched to me.

Photographs of the respective casualties came from a variety of sources. Some were found on cricket and military websites and others came from records still kept by their schools. Fellow cricket lovers passed me a few more and I then checked the painting which hangs in the entrance foyer to the pavilion and found three more; Hunt F, Stafford and Wynter. This was a fortunate discovery as images of Hunt and Stafford had proved elusive, so a painted image is a suitable substitute.

The painting features 308 members and players; there are 294 names listed on the bottom half of the key which identify those in, or in front of the pavilion and a further 14 are named towards the top of the key which identify those seated on the gallery balcony at the top of the painting. On the key next to the painting a date of 1911 is shown, along with "Charles H Parker, 17 New Oxford Street, WC", who drew up the key.

The painting depicts players such as Jack Crawford, Jack Hobbs, John Shuter and Herbert Strudwick, along with notables such as Lord Kinnaird and Colonel Richard Ridgeway VC, CB. The latter won his Victoria Cross in November 1879 aged 31 when a Captain in the Bengal Staff Corps, Indian Army and 44th Gurkha Rifles. During the Naga Hills Expedition whilst under heavy fire, he ran to a barricade and tried to rip down its protection to gain entry. It was whilst doing this that he was badly wounded.

I spent an enjoyable summer's day driving around South London photographing war memorials and graves, which I hope adds some colour to the biographies. Another trip took me to Arundel and Selsey to photograph more of the same and I made trips to Chipstead in Surrey and Stevenage to photograph a church window and a plaque. A year later I zig-zagged across Gloucestershire and Oxfordshire to photograph three more memorials, which racked up more miles. It has been a worthwhile effort to get these various memorials collected together, but I feel certain that there are a few more out there. Likewise I am sure that in old local newspapers there will be photographs of those casualties whose images have eluded me. But deadlines are deadlines.

In the first decade of the new millennium I wrote three books on cricketers buried in Belgium, France, Germany and Holland who had been killed in the Great War and the graves of four Surrey cricketers, Chinnery H, Gillespie, Myers and Raphael, were featured. But there is only one Surrey CCC first-team player killed in the Great War who is buried in England – Esme Chinnery.

Only four of those listed on the memorial are definitely buried in England: Chinnery E, Parkes, Snell and Thorne, although it is almost certain that Burrell is too, but his grave is yet to be traced by the CWGC. He has strong links to Northumberland and despite dying in Bath, it is highly likely that his body went north for burial.

On August 5th 2005 the two war memorials at Lord's cricket ground were re-dedicated and a small brochure was issued to those who attended the ceremony. The brochure states: "When research was being undertaken in order to compile a list of Members who fell in World War Two, it was decided simultaneously to examine the names recorded on the World War One Roll. Of the 329 names which had been listed, 38 should not have been included. In addition, there were 26 Members who had been excluded from the Roll. These findings were not particularly surprising, since many memorials - especially those which comprise large numbers of names - erected soon after the end of World War One have been found to contain errors of a similar nature."

Any errors can be forgiven due to the ongoing carnage and huge loss of life. In the Great War, Germany had 2.4 million prisoners-of-war and at least 552 British officers were killed (shot or beaten to death) in prisoner-of-war camps in Germany.

With regard to the war memorial on which this book focuses, I have found only a few errors and they relate to rank (either an incorrect one or its complete omission) and a name that is not in alphabetical order.

Even the most knowledgeable of Surrey CCC members, players and staff would probably be familiar with only two or three of those listed on the memorial; and Marshal and Raphael would be probably amongst these. I therefore hope that what my two years of research have unearthed adds much to the knowledge of those who read this book and brings the names and their achievements to the attention of a wider and contemporary audience. "The 48" deserve it.

Philip Paine

● ●

In Memoriam

			LT. COL.
		LEWIS, R.P.	2ND LIEUT.
	2ND LIEUT.	LONGTON, E.J.	
ALDRICH, C.P.G.	SERGT.	MARSHAL, ALAN	2ND LIEUT.
ATTWATER, E.	SEGT.MAJ.	MAY, H.G.	CPL.
BLACKLIDGE, H.G.	CAPT.	MYERS, E.B.	CAPT.
BURRELL, W.M.		NASON, J.W.W.	2ND LIEUT.
CATTLEY, H.R.	CAPT.	NIGHTINGALE, F.L.	2ND LIEUT.
CHINNERY, E.F.	LIEUT.	NOAKES, H.T.	CAPT.
CHINNERY, H.B.	CAPT.	PARKER, E.D.	CAPT.
COOPER, C.S.	CAPT.	PARKES, H.R.	LIEUT.
CURWEN, W.J.H.	2ND LIEUT.	READ, A.B.	LANCE CPL.
DAWSON, W.L.	MAJOR,	REAY, W.F.	LIEUT.
FORSTER, H.M.	LIEUT.	RAPHAEL, J.E.	2ND LIEUT.
GILL, W.G.O.	CAPT.	ROBARTS, F.W.	LIEUT.
GILLESPIE, F.S.		SCOTT, E.A.,M.C.	CAPT.
GIPPS, P.N.		SHRAPNEL, V.G.F.	2ND LIEUT.
GREEN, C.	LIEUT.	SILLS, C.C.	LIEUT.
HICKMAN, A.K.		SNELL, C.	CAPT.
HOARE, C.M.	CAPT.	STAFFORD, T.C.	LIEUT.
HOLLOWAY, B.H.	2ND LIEUT.	THORNE, A.B.	LIEUT.
HOWELL, JOHN	Q.M.S.	TUFNELL, C.W.	
HUNT, F.L.	2ND LIEUT.	WHITTLE, W.V.P.C.	
HUNT, J.H.	2ND LIEUT.	WORMALD, GUY	CAPT.
JEWELL, D.M.H.	LIEUT.	WYNTER, P.C.	CAPT.
LANE-JOYNT, A.W.	LIEUT.		
WALPOLE, H.S.			

1914-1918

THEY PLAYED
THE GAME

The memorial in the Long Room at The Oval.

The Surrey Historical Centre in Woking holds many excellent documents detailing the inner workings of Surrey CCC along with numerous old committee minute books that hold the main Committee minutes, the Finance Committee minutes and the Ground Committee minutes, all of which between them provide an invaluable record of the club's internal workings at the time. Perhaps the most interesting artefact is the huge Committee Minutes volume for 1910-19, which is under the numerical reference of 2042. It is a fascinating and detailed compilation and covers a multitude of topics about the club and its members and players.

Below are verbatim some minutes relevant to the war memorial (pictured on the previous page), that illustrate how the topic was reported and progressed.

THE COMMITTEE VOLUME

January 16th 1919 (page 315/20) – "The question of a Surrey Cricketers' memorial at The Oval was deferred."

February 20th 1919 (page 319/31) – "The question of a Surrey Cricketers' memorial at the Oval was deferred."

November 20th 1919 (page 362/13) – Under a title of "War memorial" is reported: "It was decided that a War Memorial to those who fell in the War should be provided, to include Amateur and Professional players of the first and second XIs, whether Members of the Club or not, Members of the Staff and Members of the Club, and that it be referred to the Ground Committee to report on appropriate form of memorial, estimate cost and where it shall be placed."

THE FINANCE COMMITTEE VOLUME

July 17th 1919 (page 196) – The club submitted a claim to the War Department for £3,989 – 4s – 3d for "damage and repairs rendered necessary in consequence of The Oval being a Military occupation during the war." Mr WW Dearle surveyor to the club also attended this meeting.

THE GROUND COMMITTEE VOLUME

December 12th 1919 (page 27) – "The Secretary was authorised to write to Messrs Samuel Elliott and Sons Ltd, of Reading on Mr CF Tufnell's recommendation - asking for designs and estimates and for an appointment at The Oval with a view to advise as to the most suitable position for the Memorial. Certain of the

Committee undertook to visit Burlington House where designs are on view."

January 13th 1920 (page 28) – "Estimates and drawings were presented for a cenotaph ranging in price from £135 to £375 and for oak tablets from £27 to £35 all without lettering.

The following recommendations were made:

1. That the Memorial take the form of a tablet and that it shall be placed in a suitable position inside the Pavilion.

2. That the tablet be of as plain a character as possible, oak or mahogany preferred.

3. That Messrs Elliott of Reading be further communicated with and taken into consultation on the matter of a tablet."

March 16th 1920 (page 29) – "Further drawings and Estimates from Messrs Elliott were presented and discussed. The matter was postponed for future consideration."

May 31st 1920 (page 31) – "The Secretary reported that since the issue of the Annual Report a certain number of names of those who had fallen had been added to the list. It was recommended that the Memorial Tablet be proceeded with at once."

August 16th 1920 (page 32) – "The General Committee having on January 15th directed that this matter be proceeded with, the Acting Secretary was authorised to instruct Messrs Elliott of Reading to put the Memorial in hand as per their design No 10035 and their letter of 15th March 1920, at a cost of £96.10.0 (96 pounds and 10 shillings). The question of lettering to be left to Mr CF Tufnell and the Acting Secretary."

It is interesting to note that the memorial was discussed by three separate committees and

that the cost would be £27-£35, yet the bill for its completion, after engraving, was £96.10.00. This sum is almost twice as much as the average widow's war pension for a year in 1920. Many war memorials across the country are elaborately designed, graphic, made of stone and would have been very expensive. The club's wish was for a design "of as plain a character as possible, oak or mahogany preferred." Without doubt they got their wish at a surprisingly substantial cost.

. . . .

These details are reasonably easy to find and show quite a wide geographical spread. Naturally there is a concentration in London and the Home Counties but the North of England is represented, as are further flung parts of the Empire. I have listed the counties that the 48 were born in as they were described at the time. Of course boundaries have since changed and some counties such as Middlesex have been abolished.

PLACE OF BIRTH

CHESHIRE – 1

ESSEX – 1

GLOUCESTERSHIRE – 1

KENT – 5

LANCASHIRE – 1

LONDON – 15

MIDDLESEX – 2

NORTHUMBERLAND – 2

SURREY – 10

SUSSEX – 3

WARWICKSHIRE – 1

AUSTRALIA – 1

BELGIUM – 1

IRELAND – 2

SOUTH AFRICA – 1

UNKNOWN – 1

Obtaining details of which schools the casualties attended has proved much more challenging than I'd expected. *Wisden Almanack* often shows these in their obituary section, but many of the casualties featured in this book were not players, just members of the club. Occasionally schools are mentioned in the military obituaries and some researchers on military websites have been able to obtain these details, but in the case of 14 casualties, the school they attended remains unknown.

I had expected that a small selection of schools would feature prominently and that they would be located around London and Surrey, but this was not entirely the case. Most schools will be familiar, but there are some unexpected inclusions and also some a long way from Kennington. Nevertheless, it is notable that of all the schools that I have managed to link with a casualty, all but two are existing public schools. While it is for the cultural and social historian to establish whether this ratio of privileged upbringing to casualty rate represents an anomaly, what is clear is that the membership and playing staff of Surrey CCC was drawn at the time from a disproportionately wealthy sector of society.

ETON – 5

DULWICH COLLEGE – 4

CHARTERHOUSE, HARROW, MERCHANT TAYLOR'S, SHERBORNE AND WINCHESTER – 2

CLIFTON, FELSTED, HAILEYBURY, LEYS, MILL HILL, OSBORNE, RADLEY, REPTON, SOUTH BRISBANE, UNIVERSITY SCHOOL (HASTINGS), UPPINGHAM, WELLINGTON, WESTMINSTER, WHITGIFT AND WILSON'S – 1

The above total 34. It has not been possible to find the schools that the other 14 casualties attended.

Richard Webster, 1st Viscount Alverstone – President of Surrey CCC from 1895-1915.

There is plenty of information about the rank the casualty held at the time of his death, although the Surrey war memorial does differ occasionally from records held by the Commonwealth War Graves Commission (CWGC). Again this can be accounted for by the rapid promotion of some and this fact often not being recorded for all parties. Some ranks are frustratingly not shown on the war memorial, and in the case of my nemesis – from a research perspective – C Green, this information would have narrowed down the number of possible suspects as to his true identity.

The majority of the casualties were educated at public school so it comes as no surprise that 40 of them (87%) were Commissioned Officers. All bar two of the casualties were in the Army at the time of their death, however Noakes and Tufnell kept their Army rank despite being killed whilst in the Royal Flying Corps.

RANKS AT DEATH

LIEUTENANT COLONEL – 1	SERGEANT – 1
MAJOR – 1	QUARTER MASTER SERGEANT – 1
CAPTAIN – 13	CORPORAL – 1
LIEUTENANT – 13	LANCE CORPORAL – 1
SECOND LIEUTENANT – 12	PRIVATE – 2
SERGEANT MAJOR – 1	UNKNOWN – 1

WG Grace, the original superstar of English cricket and a teammate of Alan Marshal for the Gentlemen of England.

With the exception of one man, the elusive C Green, it has been possible to establish the places of burial, or location of the war memorial on which they are remembered for all of the casualties.

There are however a few problems. Marshal was taken ill in Turkey and transferred to Malta where he was treated, died and was buried and others may also be buried or commemorated far from where they fell, were taken ill, or were last seen alive. William Burrell was taken ill at Southampton, died at Bath, yet had strong family links with Northumberland, but to date it has not been possible to locate his grave. A relative has informed me that he is buried in Northumberland, so I have shown him as being buried in England.

Whilst the geographic spread reflects the enormous reach of the Great War from Europe to the Middle East, the vast majority were buried or memorialised in France and Belgium. Perhaps more unusually, over 10% were buried in England.

COUNTRY	TOTAL	BURIED	ON A MEMORIAL
France	22	15	7
Belgium	11	8	3
England	5	5	0
Greece	2	1	1
India	2	1	1
Iraq	2	1	1
Israel	1	1	0
Malta	1	1	0
Turkey	1	0	1
Unknown	1	0	0

Morice Bird – Surrey CCC Captain 1911 - 1913.

The table shows the dates the casualties died and their relationship to the club.

Surname	Initials	Relationship to Surrey CCC	Died
Hoare	CM	Member	24/08/1914
Read	AB	Member and player	16/09/1914
Sills	CC	Player	26/09/1914
Tufnell	CW	Player	06/11/1914
Gipps	RN	Member	07/11/1914
Burrell	WM	Member	10/11/1914
Chinnery	EF	Player	18/01/1915
Parker	ED	Member	20/03/1915
May	HG	Player	27/03/1915
Whittle	WVPC	Member	13/04/1915
Wynter	PC	Member and player	20/04/1915
Curwen	WJH	Member and player	09/05/1915
Longton	EJ	Member	06/06/1915
Cooper	GS	Member	28/06/1915
Marshal	A	Player	23/07/1915
Forster	HM	Member and player	16/09/1915
Howell	J	Member and player	25/09/1915
Holloway	BH	Member and player	27/09/1915
Reay	WF	Player	28/09/1915
Robarts	FW	Member and player	13/10/1915
Nightingale	FL	Player	19/12/1915
Jewell	DMH	Player	20/01/1916
Lane-Joynt	AW	Member and player	26/02/1916
Stafford	TC	Player	04/04/1916
Hickman	AK	Member and player	05/04/1916

Surname	Initials	Relationship to Surrey CCC	Died
Scott	EA	Member	08/04/1916
Chinnery	HB	Member and player	28/05/1916
Gillespie	FS	Member and player	18/06/1916
Snell	C	Unknown	14/07/1916
Wormald	G	Member and player	14/09/1916
Myers	EB	Player	15/09/1916
Hunt	JH	Member, player and committee	16/09/1916
Aldrich	CPG	Member	07/10/1916
Nason	JWW	Member	26/12/1916
Cattley	HP	Member	14/03/1917
Gill	WGO	Player	27/03/1917
Blacklidge	HG	Player	23/05/1917
Raphael	JE	Member and player	11/06/1917
Noakes	HT	Member	23/07/1917
Lewis	RP	Member and player	07/09/1917
Attwater	E	Player	29/09/1917
Dawson	WL	Member	03/12/1917
Shrapnel	VGF	Unknown	23/03/1918
Walpole	HS	Player	09/04/1918
Thorne	AB	Player	08/05/1918
Hunt	FL	Member, player and committee	16/05/1918
Parkes	HR	Member and player	28/05/1920
Green	C	Unknown	

Below are the numbers of casualties month by month, regardless of year.

January	–	2
February	–	1
March	–	5
April	–	6
May	–	6
June	–	4
July	–	3
August	–	1
September	–	11
October	–	2
November	–	3
December	–	3
Unknown	–	1

Charles Pelham Gardner Aldrich

Second Lieutenant, Royal Fusiliers.

Died October 7th 1916, age 21.

Buried in Australian Imperial Forces Burial Ground, Flers, Somme, France.

Aldrich was born in mid-1895, in Huyton, Lancashire, the son of Charles Roper Aldrich of Westerfield Hall, Ipswich, Suffolk.

He did not play any first-class cricket and does not appear in any matches for other Surrey teams. He is shown in the 1913 edition as a schoolboy member and the following year as a full member, thus showing that full club membership could, after all, be obtained before the age of 21.

Some of those who feature in this book, for example Longton and Sills, died even younger, so were only ever schoolboy members of the club; a poignant illustration of the terrible tragedies that befell so many young men and their families during the war.

Aldrich is not listed on the war memorial in Ipswich, but on a visit to Caius College in Cambridge I found his name on the war memorial located in the foyer area of the college chapel, which was an unexpected discovery.

Details about Aldrich's brief life are in short supply but Caius College was able to send me a short biography that they have kept on him. In it we discover that: "[Aldrich] was educated first at Seafield School, Bexhill. He then went to Eastbourne College where he was head of Gonville House and was admitted to Gonville and Caius College in 1914. Charles resided for one year and intended to proceed to the Mechanical Sciences tripos having passed the qualifying mathematics examination. He does not appear in the Caian [the college magazine] as playing any sports or as a member of any club during his brief residence. He applied for a commission in the infantry or the engineers on the 25th May 1915 and his application states that he had spent nine months in the mechanical engineering laboratories at Cambridge. Whilst at College, he had been a member of the OTC (Officer Training Corps)."

It continues: "On the 29th June 1915, Charles was gazetted a temporary 2nd Lieutenant and then joined the newly formed 26th Battalion, the Royal Fusiliers, the Bankers Battalion. The battalion had trained initially at Aldershot and at 3am on the 5th May 1916, they travelled by train to Southampton and sailed for Le Havre on the SS Mona Queen. Their first spell in the trenches took place near Piggeries on the 5th June. Charles joined them on the 16th July according to his medals card. He was killed in one of the later actions of the Battle of the Somme, the attack on Bayonet Trench near Flers. It was their first experience of battle. They had moved to the Somme area in August close to Delville Wood. At the end of September, Thiepval was taken and a follow up action was planned. The weather was awful and the river was in spate. It rained almost every day and the attack was postponed. Because the men were soaked to the skin and bogged down by the mud, there was significant illness.

"The 26th moved up near Gueudecourt on the night of the 4/5th October and attacked Bayonet Trench on the 7th. This was the action in which Charles was to die. The Fusiliers were under heavy machine gun fire but held the trench until the 9th October in the last action of the battalion on the Somme.

"Charles' officer's record describes him as very tall and dark and wearing pince-nez. He was posted missing initially but a report came in from A G Rickard to confirm his death. Rickard wrote that Charles was next to him as Rickard lay wounded. Charles lay where he fell and did not move for several hours until Rickard was fetched away."

There is a short obituary in the December 8th 1916 edition of *The Times* under a sub-title "Killed in Action" which reads: "Officially reported missing, believed killed, unofficially reported killed in action Oct. 7th Charles Pelham Gardner Aldrich, second Lieutenant, Royal Fusiliers, only son of Mr. and Mrs. Charles Roper Aldrich, High Ridge, The Drive, Wimbledon, aged 21."

The cemetery in which Aldrich is buried is usually known by its shortened name of the AIF Burial Ground and it holds 3,555 casualties, although only 402 are Australians. There are 2,811 British casualties within its walls, along with 163 French, 84 New Zealanders and 27 South Africans. It is one of the bigger cemeteries that are looked after by the CWGC and is an area whose very name speaks so evocatively of the Great War – the Somme. The Australian Imperial Forces held the front line in this area during the winter of 1916 and it was first used as a burial ground in November 1916. It continued to be so only until 1917, which serves to show the stupendous speed at which casualties mounted.

•••••••••••••••••••••••••••••••••••••

AIF Burial Ground, Flers, Somme, France.

Aldrich is buried is this cemetery which contains over three thousand Commonwealth casualties, as well as some French and German ones, all from the Great War, although two-thirds of the Commonwealth graves are unidentified. His cream headstone is embossed with the badge of The Royal Fusiliers, but for those whose headstone does not show their name "Known unto God" is engraved thereon.

Ernest Attwater

Second Lieutenant, Machine Gun Corps.

Died March 22nd 1918, age 29.

Buried in Foucaucourt Communal Cemetery, Somme, France.

Ernest Attwater was born in early 1888, in Church Street, Cuckfield, Sussex, the son of Alfred and Francis of Murston, Kent.

He hailed from a large family boasting six sons and three daughters and was a whitesmith by trade. Whilst at Cuckfield he was a bell ringer (as were his five brothers) and, alongside his brothers Louis and Frank, a member of the Ancient Society of College Youths, the premier bell ringing society based in the City of London. Active in his local community he sang in the church choir and was a well-known member of the football and cricket clubs.

In *A Small Town at War* by Alan Miller, published in 1999, Attwater's marriage to Alice Ethel Hulls at Arundel church gets a mention on page 33: "Sergeant Ernest Attwater married Miss Alice Ethel Hulls at the Arundel Parish Church. The bridegroom was a well-known local athlete and before the outbreak of war was a professional cricketer with Surrey. The bride was the only daughter of Mr and Mrs Hall of Arundel. Her father was a former Mayor of Arundel. Ernest went to France with the Royal Sussex Regiment on September 1st 1915 and took part in the Loos, Ypres and Somme campaigns. He was in England at this time training for a commission.

It was offered to him in recognition of his meritorious service. He was a member of the Machine Gun Corps."

When war broke out Attwater left his duties as ground bowler to Surrey CCC and enlisted in the 58th Company of the Machine Gun Corps, receiving his attestation papers from a major in the Royal Sussex Regiment on 10th September. He was posted to 9th Battalion, one of the newly raised battalions of Kitchener's New Army and became Private 3305, but with his prior experience in the Territorial Force, for whom he had served three years prior to the war, he was promoted lance corporal as early as 12th October. He had given his profession as "carpenter and professional cricketer."

There is a photograph of him in a bell-ringing magazine called *Ringing World*, dated July 31st 1914, just four days before Britain declared war. In the magazine is an article about a cricket match between the College Youths and Cumberlands at Mitcham Green, London. Attwater took 2-19 for the College Youths in a losing cause as the Cumberlands, who scored only 33, won by two runs. (It was their first fixture for 30 years, so perhaps they can be forgiven for a certain rustiness).

He played for Surrey Club and Ground in 1913, Young Players of Surrey in 1913, Young Amateurs in 1913 and 1914 and for the Young Professionals in 1913 and 1914, his seemingly inevitable progress towards the first-team being cruelly thwarted by the war.

In reporting his death, the *Mid Sussex Times* stated that he was "a young man of sterling character and very popular in Haywards Heath as well as Cuckfield." He had seen fighting at Ypres, Loos and the Somme.

In *Cuckfield Remembered* by Shirley Bond, published in 2007, a handbill is reproduced regarding a memorial service on May 5th 1918 which included Attwater. A church bell peel to his memory is also mentioned and on page 84 there is a photograph of him and his obituary taken from the *Mid Sussex Times*.

Foucaucourt, where he is buried, is a village about 10 miles southeast of Albert on the road from Amiens to St Quentin. It was in German hands from March 26th to August 27th 1918. In the cemetery are the graves of one British soldier buried by the enemy in March 1918 (which is Attwater) and seven buried by their comrades later in the year, so he is one of only eight war casualties in this cemetery.

He is listed on at least four war memorials; two in Cuckfield (one in the churchyard and one in the church), the war memorial in Arundel town centre, where his widow Ethel moved, and of course the Surrey CCC memorial.

After the war Ethel re-married a Mr Light and moved to 4 Fitzalan Terrace, Arundel, Sussex.

•••••••••••••••••••••••••••••••••••••

This marvellous photograph comes from *Ringing World's* article on the match between The College Youths and The Cumberlands at Mitcham Green which took place just four days before the outbreak of war. Attwater can be seen directly behind the glum looking lady wearing a boater, seated in the front row. She had had a tough day – as scorer she had recorded 20 wickets and seen only 64 runs scored.

Cuckfield War Memorial, Sussex.

Attwater features on at least four war memorials. This one can be found in the churchyard of Holy Trinity Church, Cuckfield.

Henry George Blacklidge

Sergeant Major, Hampshire Regiment.

Died May 23rd 1917, age 33.

Buried in Amara War Cemetery, Iraq.

Blacklidge was born in mid-1884 in Stoughton, Surrey, just north of Guildford and was the son of John and Jean, of 2 Rosamond Villas, Church Path, East Sheen, London. He was christened at St John's Church, Stoke-next-Guildford on August 17th 1884.

In the 1901 census he is aged 16 and a "gardener-domestic" at Winterfold Gardens, Cranleigh, Surrey, one of four servants at the address.

He is one of only eight casualties listed on the memorial to have played first-class cricket for Surrey. He played for the Surrey Club and Ground XI in 1906 and between 1908 and 1913, for Cranleigh in 1911 and for the Surrey second XI between 1906 and 1913. His first appearance for the first XI was against Gentlemen of Philadelphia at The Oval in July 1908. He scored 14 and 12*, took 1-49 and 4-26 and held one catch as Surrey won by 122 runs. In the Surrey XI was Alan Marshal, who also features in this book.

His debut for Surrey in the County Championship came against Essex at Leyton in August 1908 when he scored 45 and took three wickets in the drawn match. He played twice more that season;

against Gloucestershire at Bristol and Somerset at Bath. His next Championship appearance did not come until May 1912 when he played against Gloucestershire at The Oval and batting at No.8 scored four runs and took 0-36 in the match. Surrey won the match convincingly by an innings and 87 runs. His second match of the season was against Nottinghamshire at the same ground and his final Championship match was in May 1913 against Warwickshire, again at The Oval. He bowed out with 6*, one wicket and two catches in a drawn match.

He played a total of seven first-class matches, six of which were for Surrey in the County Championship in a career lasting from July 1908 to May 1913 and scored 100 runs in nine innings, took 10 wickets for 344 and held eight catches. He was a left-handed batsman and shown as both a slow left-arm orthodox and a left-arm fast-medium bowler.

Committee minute notes relating to a meeting on July 18th 1912 show he was granted winter wages from September 1912 to March 1913 whilst undertaking a coaching role in Buenos Aires, Argentina. On page 159 of the same volume, minutes relating to a committee meeting on October 16th 1913 stated: "Leave was granted to HG Blacklidge to accept an engagement with Derbyshire CCC in 1914."

Blacklidge played for Derbyshire's second XI in 1914 and was also qualifying for Hampshire. Sadly, any future he may have had with either of these counties was extinguished by the declaration of war in August 1914.

He was sent to Gallipoli and then the Middle East but, like so many casualties in the Great War, he died not on the battlefield but instead from dysentery, in Iraq.

As for his burial location, CWGC records say: "Amara is on the left bank of the Tigres river and became a hospital centre...... Unfortunately in 1933 all of the headstones were removed when it was discovered that salts in the soil were causing them to deteriorate. Instead a screen wall was erected with the names of those buried in the cemetery engraved upon it."

His obituary in the 1918 *Wisden Almanack* succinctly records: "Born at Stoughton, Surrey, July 14, 1884, died of dysentery in Mesopotamia in May. Surrey 1912 and 1913; Surrey 2nd XI; was qualifying for Hampshire at outbreak of the War. Useful all-round; fast bowler."

....

This photograph of Blacklidge was taken in 1908 by the famous cricket photographer Hawkins, whose material is still highly sought after by collectors. The Hawkins studio at 32 Preston Street, Brighton was established about 1861 by Charles Hawkins (1825-1871) and after his death was run by his widow Eliza.

Claygate War Memorial, Surrey.

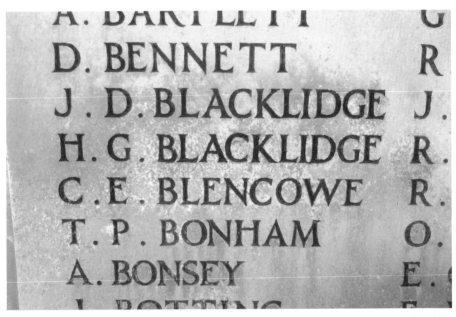

Blacklidge and his brother are both listed on this impressive war memorial located in a central position in the market town of Claygate, although his name is not to be found on any memorials in the church.

William Matthew Burrell

Major, Northumberland Hussars Yeomanry.

Died November 10th 1914, age 38.

Place of burial not known.

Burrell was born on February 2nd 1876 in Glen Allen, Alnwick, Northumberland and educated at Harrow School. He married Nancy Perkins of Hampton Court, Leominster, Herefordshire on May 13th 1903 and they had four children.

He is one of the few listed on the war memorial who was a career soldier and one whose army details are worth outlining in more detail. He was gazetted Second Lieutenant in the Royal Lancers on May 15th 1897, promoted to Lieutenant in 1900 and to Captain on November 22nd 1902. He served in the Boer War between 1899 and 1902, taking part in the relief of Kimberley, and saw further action at Maggersfontein in the Orange Free State between February and May 1900, in Transvaal between May and June 1900, west of Pretoria between July and November 1900 and in the Cape Colony between July 1901 and May 1902. He was awarded the Queen's Medal with four clasps and the King's Medal with two clasps, eventually retiring on May 15th 1907. Thereafter he joined the Northumberland Yeomanry Hussars where he was adjutant for three years before being promoted to Major on June 7th 1913. This rank differs from the one shown on the memorial, so along with Forster he is the second highest ranking casualty of our

48; only Lewis at Lieutenant-Colonel attained a higher rank.

On the 1911 census he is shown as residing at Carham Hall, Coldstream, Northumberland with his wife Nancy, daughter Cornelia and 14 servants. Sadly another child had already died.

He did not play any first-class cricket, but was a member of the club in 1912 and shown as Capt. WM Burrell.

The history of his regiment states: "...was succeeded by Captain WM Burrell (12th Royal Lancers), who thus continued a family connection with the regiment dating back to the time of Colonel Bryan Burrell, who was in command from 1871 to 1876. Captain Burrell remained as adjutant until 1907. Leaving the regular army, he was commissioned to the Northumberland Hussars, and he continued to serve with the rank of major. He died in 1914, just prior to embarkation of the regiment for France."

Currently there is no trace of his death amongst the CWGC records, although this oversight has been brought to their attention. At the outbreak of war he was en route to France when he was taken ill with pneumonia at Southampton and died at 19 Somerset Place, Bath on November 10th 1914. As a result he is classed as a war death, although not yet included as such on CWGC records. His regiment sailed from Southampton to Zeebrugge on October 5th 1915.

His will shows him living at Broome Park, Northumberland and he left effects of £14,279 – 3s – 3d to his widow Nancy. This would have represented an enormous estate, equivalent in today's terms to around £3 million.

A probate record hints that he may be buried in Northumberland and a relative of his stated that he is buried in Bolton Chapel, near Alnwick in Northumberland.

Burrell represents something of an outlier in this book in that he was born nowhere near The Oval, spent much of his life abroad, played no cricket for any representative Surrey team and was only a member for one year. Furthermore, although he is one of only two of our 48 to achieve the rank of Major, he saw no action in the Great War and died on English soil.

••••••••••••••••••••••••••••••••••••

St Mary's Church, Hope-under-Dinmore, Herefordshire.

This impressive and very shiny war memorial for the village is inside the local church, located on the A49 road. It is close to Hampton Court Castle where Burrell's bride lived, although according to staff at the church, there are no memorials to Burrell. He was taken ill at Southampton, died at Bath, is likely to be buried in Northumberland and has this memorial commemorating him in Herefordshire.

Burrell was a career soldier and in 16 years rose through the ranks from Lieutenant to Major. He died leaving a widow and three children aged between two months and three-and-a-half years. His first child was born in 1909, but died aged just six months.

Hubert Pennington Cattley

Private, Manchester Regiment.

Died March 14th 1917, age 26.

Buried in Gommecourt, British Cemetery No.2, Hebuterne, Pas de Calais, France.

Cattley was born in late 1890 in Brighton, Sussex and is one of two Privates listed on the memorial; the other being the very talented cricketer Alan Marshal.

In the 1911 census he was 20, living in Mannings Hill, Cranleigh, Surrey, with sister Marjorie and mother Lilian, aged 47 and shown as head of the family. Three servants are also shown residing at the address.

In the 1899 club yearbook HT, MC, MH, SW and Wildman Cattley, family members on his father's side, are all listed as members of the club. There is no first name, age or next-of-kin shown for him in the CWGC records, although his mother lived at 17 Hyde Park Terrace, London W1. The Surrey CCC yearbooks show that he was a member of the club from 1907-14.

He did not play any first-class cricket, but Arthur Cattley (1861-1895) played for Surrey in 1882, Stephen Wildman Cattley (1860-1925) for Surrey between 1879 and 1883 and a W Cattley (dates of birth and death and first name not known) for Surrey between 1857 and 1858.

Before hostilities began he was a bank clerk. On September 25th 1914 he enlisted for action at St James's and joined the Middlesex Regiment where his service number was 1018. He was sent to France on November 19th 1915 and transferred to the 22nd Manchester's (service number 44321) on November 1st 1916.

Cattley's great-niece informed me that he was educated at Eton and later Merton College, Oxford University and that his grandparents were radical Liberals. His long-lived grandfather, Frederick Pennington (1819-1914) was the Liberal MP for Stockport from 1874-85 and his grandmother, Margaret, was a Suffragette. She adds that Hubert is mentioned on the war memorials at the Reform Club in London and Eton School. This casualty is a good example of the family name being continued by its use as a middle-name for offspring. Most unusually for an alumnus of Eton and Oxford, he only obtained the rank of Private, despite his three years' service.

Family probate records show: "Hubert Pennington Cattley - 24th December 1917 - of 17 Hyde Park Terrace, Middx killed 14th March 1917 in France on active service. Administration London 24th December 1917 to Lilian Cattley widow. Effects sworn at £154 – 18s – 9d."

Gommecourt British Cem. No 2, Hebuterne, France.

Cattley is interred in this rural cemetery about 13 miles southwest of Arras with 1,356 others, about half of whom are in unnamed graves. In keeping with tradition the badge of his regiment is on his headstone. There are four cemeteries in very close proximity named Gommecourt British Cemeteries No.1, No.2, No.3 and No.4. They were constructed in 1917 when the battlefields were cleared. After the Armistice, graves from the neighbouring battlefields were added.

Esme Fairfax Chinnery

Captain, Royal Flying Corps.

Died January 18th 1915, age 28.

Buried in St Matthew's Church, Hatchford, Surrey.

Chinnery was born on March 28th 1886 in Hatchford, Surrey, the son of Walter, DL, JP, and Alice. Walter had been an excellent runner and held the world amateur record for the mile (four minutes 29 seconds) for many years, but died suddenly in 1905, aged just 61.

Chinnery was educated at Eton from January 1900 to February 1905, where records show that he was under the tutelage of Miss Evans and was "Keeper of Rackets" from 1904-05. He represented the school first XI cricket team in 1904 and 1905. On June 24th 1904 he opened the batting for Eton against Winchester and scored 24 and 0 as his side lost by eight wickets and he played against Harrow and Winchester the following season.

On April 25th, aged just 14, he opened the batting for the misleadingly named HO Dolbey's XI (who had 16 players) against J Wormald's XI at The Oval. In April 1902 he played for J Wormald's XI against WT Graburn's XI at the same ground and scored 14 batting at number 7 and took 0-11 off 2 overs, as the opposition won by 4 wickets.

In 1907 Chinnery opened the batting with England cricket and football player Andy Ducat

for the Surrey second XI against Yorkshire second XI at Rotherham Town cricket ground, scoring five in his only visit to the crease in the drawn match. His lone first-class match for Surrey was against Oxford University in June 1906 at The Oval. Batting at No.6 he scored 47 in his only innings, as Surrey won by nine wickets.

In May 1909 he played for Household Brigade against MCC at Lord's in a single innings match, but did not get to bat (at No.6) as the match lasted just four overs before being rained off. In the corresponding match in July 1910, he batted at No.9, scoring seven and 27 and taking 0-29 as his side were thrashed by an innings and 26 runs. From 1910 he was a member of MCC.

An entry in *The London Gazette* dated July 4th 1913 states: "ROYAL FLYING CORPS. Military Wing, Lieutenant Esme F. Chinnery, Coldstream Guards, to be a Flying Officer, and to be seconded. Dated 30th. April, 1913."

He was mentioned in despatches during the Great War, commissioned whilst in the Coldstream Guards and qualified as a pilot in 1912. He died whilst a passenger in a Voisin aeroplane with Monsieur M Delporte, a French civilian test pilot who perished alongside him. He was shown as being a member of the Coldstream Guards and the Royal Flying Corps (4th Squadron). He was a Freemason and a member of the Apollo University Lodge in Oxfordshire (Number 357).

Chinnery is the only war casualty in St. Matthew's churchyard and is buried in an ornate family plot, although the church itself has been demolished. He is buried in front of his parents and next to his brother Walter, who died in 1892 aged just two days, and another brother, Ivan who died in April 1914 aged 20.

His name is on three war memorials: one at Warnham in Sussex which lists casualties in the year of their death and shows him to be a member of the Coldstream Guards and Royal Flying Corps, one at Bognor Regis Memorial Hospital in Sussex, and with Harry, his half-brother, another in the churchyard where he is buried. Harry played first-class cricket for Middlesex, MCC and Surrey.

The Sussex Daily News dated January 21st 1915 reported:

"CAPTAIN CHINNERY OF WARNHAM FATALLY BURNED IN AEROPLANE DISASTER IN FRANCE"

"By the terrible death experienced by Captain Esme Fairfax Chinnery, on the 18th January, near Issy, Sussex has lost its second exceptionally brilliant and promising airman... Captain Chinnery succumbed to his injuries shortly after 4pm on the 18th January, while flying over Paris and when near the Eiffel Tower, and his body was removed to the Valde Grace Hospital. Captain Chinnery was in a Voisin aeroplane, the pilot of which was one of the best in the employ of the Voisin Company. According to the report of an eye witness, the aeroplane was flying very low, only just skimming the roofs, when it suddenly burst into flames and fell on the quayside. In a few minutes nothing was left of the machine but a mass of red hot tangled wires and steel. The pilot was still alive when the rescuers reached the machine, but he died in hospital an hour later.

ON THE PLAYING FIELDS OF ETON

"Captain Chinnery was born in March, 1886 and was the son of the late Mr Walter Moresby Chinnery, of Hatchford Park, Cobham, and the elder and only surviving son of Mrs Christopher Stone, of Field Place, near Horsham, the birth-place of the poet Shelley. His father was a famous athlete, who was long identified with the London Athletic Club, and Captain Chinnery may be said to have inherited some of his father's high qualities in that respect. A typical Eton quick wicket batsman, he took part in that exciting Eton and Harrow match at Lord's in 1905, when play lasted until 7.30 on the Saturday; and the match had then to be declared a draw, Eton wanting 76 runs, and having only one wicket to fall. Going from Eton to Brasenose College, Oxford, he did not succeed in getting into the XI, not because he was not a good cricketer, but owing to the fact that he went up in a particularly strong year. He was, however, chosen to take part in the competitions at Queen's Club against Cambridge.

HIS ARMY CAREER

"He was gazetted a Second-Lieutenant in the Coldstream Guards in August, 1910, and promoted Lieutenant in July, 1911. In 1913 he joined the military wing of the Royal Flying Corps, and, as Flight Commander, received the temporary rank of Captain on 4th September, 1914. That his loss is a serious one will be felt by all who knew him. Tall and fair, and personally a most charming man, he has been described as one of the most brilliant members of the Royal Flying Corps who gave up a promising career on land to take the risks of the air service. He was well-known as a skilful and experienced airman, and was one of the first six men of the Corps to land in France in August last. During the retreat from the north to the Marne he did splendid work as an observer for both the French and British armies."

The same newspaper dated January 22nd 1915 reported:

"THE LATE CAPTAIN CHINNERY
MEMORIAL SERVICE AT WARNHAM"

"The mortal remains of Captain and Flight-Commander Esme Fairfax Chinnery, whose death occurred near Paris on the 18th January under such regrettable circumstances, were yesterday interred in France, and a memorial service was, at the same time, held at St Margaret's, Warnham, the Rev. Prebendary R Bowcott, RD, officiating. In addition to the relatives and the household at Field Place, the congregation included Mr Eric Lucas, Mrs and Miss Bowcott, Miss I. Davidson and the Misses Lee Steere."

On March 6th 1915 the same newspaper reported: "Chinnery's will (of Field Place, Horsham) valued at £16,631."

There now seems to be some confusion about his place of burial, although perhaps his remains were exhumed. Up to 1915 this practice was permitted if the family could afford it.

● ●

CAPTAIN E. F. CHINNERY,
COLDSTREAMS AND R.F.C.

This rare photograph of Chinnery was found on a memorial website and shows him in military uniform with a large, stiff collar.

Warnham War Memorial, Sussex.

Chinnery is commemorated on the war memorial at Warnham village in Sussex, which lists the casualties in order of their death and shows their respective ranks and regiments. It is in good condition, having not weathered over the years.

St Matthew's Church, Hatchford, Surrey.

Although the church has long since been demolished, its churchyard remains, but the access point via the entrance to a farm can easily be missed. Chinnery is buried in a large family plot enclosed with railings.

St Matthew's Church, Hatchford, Surrey.

Chinnery's is probably the most decorative cricketer's grave that I have ever found. The well-crafted headstone has on it the badge of The Royal Flying Corps and is engraved with: "To the glorious memory of Captain Esme Chinnery, Coldstream Guards and Royal Flying Corps beloved elder son of Walter Moresby and Alice... killed on active service in France." It was extremely rare for a war casualty killed in France to be brought home for burial.

Bognor Regis Hospital War Memorial.

More decorative work here on this attractive war memorial at Bognor Regis Hospital.

Harry Broderick Chinnery

Lieutenant, King's Royal Rifle Corps.

Died May 28th 1916, age 40.

Buried in Berles-au-Bois Churchyard extension, Pas de Calais, France.

Harry Broderick Chinnery was born on February 6th 1876 in Teddington, Middlesex and, like his half-brother Esme, was educated at Eton where he was in Mr Broadbent's class from February 1889 to February 1895.

He played cricket for the school in 1894 and 1895, won the double rackets in the same years and the single rackets in 1895 and was "Keeper of Rackets" between 1893 and 1895. In total he played 66 first-class matches between 1897 and 1910 in a stop-start career that was frequently interrupted by his work at the London Stock Exchange which he joined in 1898. Initially he represented Surrey for whom he was captain occasionally in 1898 (although presumably when Kingsmill Key was absent, as he was never given the job permanently), then went on to play for Middlesex from 1899-1902, with intermittent appearances for MCC between 1897 and 1902. In 1904 he returned to Surrey for his final first class appearances. In total this reputedly stylish right-handed batsman amassed 2,536 runs at an average of 24.86, which included four centuries. In addition he took 12 wickets at 46.16 with his slow-left-arm bowling and held 25 catches. He was capped by Surrey in 1904. He scored centuries in three successive innings (two for MCC and one for Middlesex) in

1901, but was abroad for the whole of the 1903 season. He was also a member of Surrey from 1894-1904 and from 1907-1913.

In lesser matches he played for Gentlemen (1897-1898), PF Warner's XI (1897), CI Thornton's England XI (1898), AJ Webbe's XI (1900), HDG Leveson-Gower's XI (1898-1909), Gentlemen of England (1907-1910), Eton College (1894-1895), MCC (1896), I Zingari (1896), Surrey 2nd XI (1896), PF Warner's XI (1897), Lord Coventry's XI (1900) and Oxford University Authentics (1902-03). He also toured America in 1897 with Pelham Warner's XI.

The *Cricket* magazine, dated July 28th 1904, features him on the cover and begins its lengthy article about him with this flattering speculation: "if Mr. Chinnery had been able to play regularly in first-class cricket from the time that he left Eton, he would have now been among the first dozen batsmen in England. He is one of the most attractive players in England to watch, and it is remarkable that a man of his size can hit with such power." Later on in the article we learn that whilst recuperating on the island of Madeira, he played for a visiting team against "the residents", for whom he scored a century, the first ever recorded on the island.

Lest we might think this match uncompetitive the magazine clarifies that the residents "were all Englishmen".

There is a photo of Harry on the Roll-of-Honour website in relation to the Stock Exchange war memorial in London. The Stock Exchange has moved from close to Bank to near St Paul's Cathedral and the memorial is at neither of these buildings now. Wilfred Dawson, who also features in this book, was another who worked at the Stock Exchange.

Like his brother Esme, Harry was a Freemason and was a Senior Warden, Master Elect in the Verity Lodge in London (number 2739).

His long obituary in *Wisden Almanack* in 1917 states: "A stylish batsman and smart field, he was in the Eton XI in 1894 and 1895, in the latter year heading the batting averages with 45.14. In his four public school matches – against Harrow and Winchester – he scored 182 runs in six innings, his greatest triumph being to make 75 and 64 v Harrow in 1895... In 1897 he assisted Surrey and in the match with Warwickshire at Edgbaston played an innings of 149. A year later little was seen of him, but at the end of the season he scored 97 for MCC v Yorkshire at Scarborough and in 1899 began to appear for Middlesex... He was only 26 when he made his last appearance in County cricket. His early retirement was much to be regretted, but he continued to assist the Eton Ramblers and I Zingari. Since 1896 he had been a member of MCC. He was the son of the late Mr Walter Chinnery, the champion mile runner in the early days of amateur athletics."

Harry's Company Commander wrote of him: "He was in the middle of his men, encouraging them in a moment of danger. He was killed by the last shell fired at a night working party which was advancing our line nearer to the enemy. It was a trying night, and he did splendidly all the earlier part of it in keeping them at their work and keeping up their spirits." His Colonel wrote: "He will be greatly missed by his brother-officers and the men of his Company, while by his death the Battalion has lost a valuable officer whom it would be difficult to replace." Chinnery's popularity with his men may be judged by the following extracts from a letter written by a rifleman "on behalf of the fellows in his Platoon and myself". It states: "Mr. Chinnery was loved and respected by all of us that he came in contact with. While in charge of the Machine Gun Section in England, and last Autumn out here, he was looked upon as something more than a good officer and a perfect gentleman; and although he had only been with No.6 Platoon six weeks, yet no Officer was more respected and had their complete confidence. Many are the stories told by his men of his splendid courage and coolness on Sunday night (the night of his death); always first in his area to go to a wounded man, to assist and cheer with a kindly word."

He is unique of those listed on the Surrey CCC war memorial in that he has a special memorial. It is one of two special memorials, the other being for two casualties buried in the churchyard extension whose respective plots are now unmarked as their graves were destroyed by shell-fire. His name is on the war memorial at Lord's, as he was a member of MCC, the one at Eton College and, along with his brother Esme, on the stylish memorial in the churchyard of the demolished St Matthew's Church in Hatchford, Surrey.

Photographs of Harry Chinnery are easier to come by than for his half-brother Esme. I had three to choose from and they all showed him in cricket attire.

Berles-au-Bois Churchyard, Pas de Calais, France.

Chinnery is buried in the extension of Berles-au-Bois village churchyard whose church was destroyed by shelling in the Great War. The current church now stands 400 yards away in this village, 10 miles southwest of Arras. The cemetery was begun in September 1915 and closed in January 1917. It contains 144 casualties of the Great War. Two are identified by special memorials as their headstones were destroyed by shell-fire. One of these is Chinnery's.

Esme Chinnery & Harry Chinnery

(1886-1915)   (1876-1916)

St Matthew's Church, Hatchford, Surrey.

Both Esme and Harry Chinnery are listed on this well-crafted war memorial in the village churchyard, but not in any discernible order. It is still clean and in excellent condition, having not suffered any weathering. Their respective names are at the head of each column and regiments are shown for each casualty as are any gallantry medals awarded.

Jack Crawford, a fine all-rounder for Surrey from 1904 to 1921.

George Stanley Cooper

Captain, Queen's Own (West Kent Regiment).

Died June 28th 1915, age 34.

Buried in Jhansi Cantonment Cemetery, India.

George Stanley Cooper was born in 1881 in Lewisham, Kent, the son of George and Mary. In late 1906 he married Clara Tilling in Bromley, Kent and on the 1911 census he is shown living at Highfield, Westmoreland Road, Bromley, Kent with his wife, father-in-law and other relatives by marriage.

Cooper was a pre-war Territorial Force officer and may have been in the Rifle Volunteers pre-1908. He obtained the rank of Captain in late 1908. The West Kent Regiment Territorial Officers tended on the whole to hail from established professions such as accountancy and the law. The 1911 Census shows Cooper as a "Master printer" by trade.

He did not play any first-class cricket, or for any lesser Surrey XIs, but was a member of the club in 1914. Of the 48 casualties in this book, his demise was perhaps the most notorious and shocking.

On Saturday July 3rd 1915 *The Times* reported;

"INDIAN SOLDIERS RUN AMOK.THREE
BRITISH OFFICERS KILLED"

The Press Bureau issued the following last night:

"The Government of India reports the occurrence of a lamentable tragedy in the 8th Cavalry, Indian Army, stationed at Jhansi.

"Two Mahomedan soldiers "ran amok" in the lines, shooting and killing Major Gale, and cutting down Lieutenant Courtenay, who has since died of his wounds. The murderers ran towards the officers' mess and on the way met and wounded Captain Hudson. Turning towards the Artillery Barracks they fired at a sergeant and a bombardier, wounding slightly the former, but killing the latter.

"The murderers were pursued and shot down by a party of men of the regiment led by two British officers, but not before they had fired at and killed another officer, Captain Cooper. The two men are reported to have been of a morose and fanatical disposition. They kept aloof from their comrades. The act was an isolated one, in which no one but the two murderers was involved."

I have been fortunate to be given details about Cooper from Christopher Jupp's work on the 5th Battalion of the Royal West Kent Regiment

(1914-20) in which he writes of the incident that resulted in Cooper's death: "On Monday 28th June two brothers serving in the 8th Cavalry, and wishing to remain together found that one was to serve overseas and the other was not. Their request to remain together was turned down, and this started a murderous rampage. At about 0800hrs they shot dead Major PG Gale, sabred and shot dead Lt FL Courtenay and wounded Capt & Adj Hudson of their own regiment. They then made their way to the Station Office where, en route, they shot dead a Bombardier and wounded a Sergeant of 79 Bty RFA. Captain GS Cooper, 1/5th Royal West Kent, who was acting as Station Staff Officer and was making his way to breakfast when the two Sowars [a term for an Indian cavalryman] passed, turned and promptly shot him in the back, killing him instantly. The two Sowars were then shot down by some Gunners who, on hearing the firing, had turned out, but unfortunately too late to save Captain Cooper.

"Captain George Stanley Cooper, aged 34, was buried by the Battalion in Jhansi Cantonment Cemetery, who mourned the loss of a good regimental officer, a good sportsman, thoroughly keen and very popular."

On July 30th 1915 the *Bromley & District Times* reported the following, the details having come from the stalwart Sergeant FC Fawcitt: "It appears that two of the native Sowars of the 8th Cavalry (native) had run amok, and before they were finally shot they had killed two officers and one artilleryman, and wounded two other officers and one artilleryman. One of the latter officers died in the afternoon, that making four deaths. One Sowar had a gun, the other a scimitar.

"Three of the officers belonged to the 8th Cavalry; the fourth was one of ours, Captain Cooper, of South Hill. He was Station Staff Officer at the Brigade Office. He was just going to enter the gate of his bungalow, which is almost opposite the Brigade Office, and, it is said, the men saluted him and then shot him in the back. By this time some of the officers who live next door guessed what was up, and were soon out with their revolvers, and before the Sowars could do more damage they were both riddled with bullets. Then some of their own regiment came down. We didn't know whether they had broken loose or not, but, when they saw the two dead men lying in the road they pierced them again and again with their lances. The two artillerymen who were shot, I believe, were cleaning their horses at the time.

"The Sowars were two brothers, and I believe for some time something like this had been expected. Of course there were a lot of rumours as to the cause of it. One was that a draft had been ordered to leave that day, and one brother was picked and the other wasn't. Another was that they did not want to go. However, they had some grievance, and that was the outcome of it. Captain Cooper was one of the best, and a good officer, and it is horrible to think that four good lives should be lost like that.

"The two officers, Major Gale and Captain Cooper, and the artilleryman, were buried the same evening, our battalion finding the firing party, 300 rifles. The artillery found the gun carriages, the remainder of the battalion and the artillery following behind."

The National Probate records show that his address was "Lancy, Durham Avenue, Bromley, Kent" and that his effects were administered on September 8th in London. He left an estate of £2,904 – 11s – 11d to his wife Clara Cooper.

After his death his widow married Major George Dominic Heyland, one of Cooper's fellow officers from India, and moved to Heyland's estate in Northern Ireland which CWGC records show as Ballintemple, Garvagh, County Derry, Northern Ireland.

Details about Derek, his third child (of four) were easy to track down. He was born in Bromley, Kent and joined the Army as a reservist in 1936, moving on to The Household Cavalry. He saw action at Normandy in 1944. His entry on Wikipedia records: "The family were comfortably wealthy – the Coopers family were printers, and the Tillings owned a substantial omnibus company. His father was killed in Jhansi in India in 1915, while serving with the Royal West Kent Regiment."

CWGC records show that he is listed on the Madras 1914-18 memorial in Chennai and that: "The 1914-1918 memorial is situated at the rear of the cemetery. It bears the names of more than a thousand servicemen who died during the First World War who lie in many civil and cantonment cemeteries in various parts of India where it is not possible to maintain their graves in perpetuity."

• •

Cooper was the only casualty in this book that I have established was a Territorial Force officer before joining the Army full-time. He is also the only one to have been murdered; shot in the back after being saluted by two men.

Wilfred John Hutton Curwen

Captain, Royal Fusiliers.

Died May 9th 1915, age 32.

Listed on the Menin Gate Memorial, Ypres, West Vlaanderen, Belgium.

Curwen was born on April 14th 1883 in Beckenham, Kent, the only son of the late John and Maria of The High House, Thames Ditton, Surrey. His brother-in-law was Charles Wreford-Brown (1866-1951) who played 12 matches for Oxford University between 1886 and 1889 and five for Gloucestershire between 1886 and 1898.

He was educated at Charterhouse School near Godalming in Surrey and, despite his poor academic performance, was able to matriculate as a Commoner at Magdalen College, Oxford University owing to his all-round sporting prowess. On finishing his education he enrolled with the 2nd Volunteer Battalion of the Royal Fusiliers whom he served between 1900 and 1905.

Curwen represented Charterhouse at rackets but made more of a name for himself playing football for the Corinthian Casuals. He made 12 appearances on their tour of South Africa in 1903 and went to Austria, Hungary and Scandinavia on their undefeated tour of 1904. So dominant were the Casuals in Hungary, the country that would humiliate England at Wembley in 1953 thanks to Puskas and co., that in seven victorious matches they scored 47 goals while conceding only seven.

Curwen also turned out for Old Carthusians for whom he played in their Arthur Dunn Cup Final wins of 1904-06, 1908 and 1910. For the latter, he usually played at wing-half. Whilst at Oxford he gained a blue for football in 1905 and 1906 and also played for an AFA English XI versus Bohemia in 1908 and 1909. In *History of the Corinthian FC* Norman Creek wrote: "Several of the party were musical, and Hewitt, Norris and Curwen took part in many entertainments on board the ship taking them to Gothenburg."

A right-hand batsman and right-arm medium-pace bowler Curwen played many matches opening the batting for Young Amateurs of Surrey in September 1902, during what was probably their cricket week, and also for Gentlemen of Surrey and Surrey Club and Ground. Whilst playing for the Young Amateurs he was often in the same XI as Nightingale and Wormald, both of whom also feature in this book. He played nine first-class matches for Oxford University in 1906 and 12 for MCC between 1906 and 1910, which included eight on the 1906/07 tour to New Zealand and two non-first-class matches on the 1911/12 tour to Australia. In 1909 he played four matches for the Surrey first XI, one of which was against the touring Australians. He was not only a member of Surrey (1900-09), I

Zingari, Free Foresters, Harlequins and MCC but also The Bath Club in London on which PG Wodehouse based his fictional Drones Club. When making his will, Curwen gave the club as his address and, with his moderate academic record, wealthy background and multiple sporting preoccupations, it's easy to imagine him taking on the Pongo Twistletons and Bingo Littles of his day in the annual darts tournament.

When war broke out Curwen was a Lieutenant in the London Regiment which he had joined in April 1911 and ADC to the Liberal politician the Rt. Hon. Sir RC Munro-Ferguson, Governor-General and Commander-in-Chief of the Commonwealth of Australia. He soon returned to England and was promoted to Captain in the London Regiment of The Royal Fusiliers on Christmas Day 1914, shortly afterwards being posted abroad with his regiment.

After undergoing training in Malta, Curwen landed in France on 15th March 1915. He was to die near Poperinghe in Belgium directing his men in the second battle of Ypres during the Battle of Aubers Ridge which would cost the British and Indian forces nearly 12,000 casualties. He didn't take part in the three day battle until late on the second day by which time thousands of British and Indian forces had been slaughtered by artillery and machine-gun fire. His brigade was ordered forward across 2,000 yards of open country in the teeth of German artillery fire with inevitable and tragic consequences. Curwen is one of over 54,000 to be listed on the large and impressive Menin Gate Memorial at Ypres in Belgium, as his grave is unmarked. His Commanding Officer, in writing about his death, stated: "He died bravely while doing his duty."

His good-length obituary in the 1917 *Wisden Almanack* reads: "was killed in action in France on May 13th [sic] 1915. In 1901 and 1902 he was in the Charterhouse XI, averaging 22.66 in the former year, and 26.80 in the latter. In 1901 he was second in the bowling, taking seventeen wickets for 18.23 runs each. At Oxford he obtained his blue in 1906, scoring 12 not out and 34 not out v Cambridge, and in his second innings added 90 runs in fifty-five minutes for the last wicket with E. G. Martin (56). Occasionally he appeared for Surrey, and in 1906-07 was a member of the MCC's team to New Zealand. Subsequently he went to Australia, and during 1912-13 was thus enabled to play for the MCC's team at Geelong and Ballarat. He was a good batsman and a useful fast-medium bowler."

Curwen is listed on the war memorial at Lord's along with seven others who feature in this book. He is also on the Charterhouse School war memorial and, along with Carleton Tufnell, is on the Band of Brothers war memorial at Canterbury cricket ground. He left £4,783 – 17s – 1d, all of which went to his sister, his only living relative.

• •

This photograph was taken by Foster of Brighton, the well-known photographer, and comes from a book called *With the MCC to New Zealand* by PR May which was published in 1907.

Curwen was a fine footballer who played many times for Corinthian Casuals. In this team photo of Old Carthusians FC he can be seen seated on the left end of the front row with an appropriately serious demeanour.

Medal index cards are still kept at the National Archives in Kew, London and show the medals, theatres of war and extraneous details about the many millions who served in the Great War. The one above shows, mid-way down on the left, that Curwen was entitled to the Victory Medal and 1915 Star, and on the right that he was killed in action on May 9th 1915.

Band of Brothers War Memorial, Kent CCC, Canterbury.

This large wooden war memorial is on the outside of the pavilion. Amongst the many names on it are two who are also on the Surrey CCC war memorial – Wilfred Curwen and Carleton Tufnell. To play for the exclusive Band of Brothers Cricket Club one has to have connections with Kent and be invited to join. Both were born in Kent and Tufnell's father played for the county.

Menin Gate Memorial, Ypres, West Vlaanderen, Belgium.

Curwen's name is listed under his rank (Captain) and the heading "The Royal Fusiliers" on the left-hand side. The arch was designed in 1921 by Reginald Blomfield and contains the names of nearly 55,000 casualties who have no known grave. Despite its huge size, when completed it was still not big enough to contain all the names of those with no known grave, so the names of 34,984 casualties who were missing after August 15th 1917 were inscribed on the Tyne Cot Memorial.

Lord Dalmeny, Surrey CCC Captain 1905-1907 and a pre-war teammate of John Raphael for the Gentlemen of the South.

Wilfred Leedham Dawson

Second Lieutenant, Royal Warwickshire Regiment.

Died December 12th 1917, age 35.

Listed on the Cambrai Memorial, Louverval, France.

Dawson was born in late 1882 in Wandsworth, London and is one of a good number of Lieutenants listed on the memorial, but the CWGC has scant information about him. There are no details of his age, place of residence or next-of-kin and sadly his place of burial is unmarked and unknown, so he is listed on the Cambrai War Memorial for those with no known grave.

Further research however shows his parents were William and Mary and that he was baptised in All Saints Church, Clapham Park on October 7th 1882. His father was a stockbroker.

He did not play any first-class cricket, nor apparently any lower level cricket for the county, but the yearbooks show that he was a member of the club from 1907-14.

Like Harry Chinnery, he worked at the Stock Exchange and details in their memorial book state that he joined in 1913. He was a partner in Bragg, Stockdale, Hall and Company. He then enlisted in the Artist's Rifles, was commissioned in 1916 and went to France on being gazetted, but died whilst holding the line near La Vacquerie.

His will shows his address as 6 Birdhurst Rise, Croydon, Surrey and effects of £2,516 – 1s –

10d, a considerable sum in those days. His executors, who were both shown as "Gentlemen" were William and Bernard Dawson.

The CWGC website states: "The Cambrai War Memorial commemorates more than seven thousand servicemen of the United Kingdom and South Africa who died in the Battle of Cambrai in November and December 1917 and whose graves are not known. The proposed method of assault was new; tanks would be used to break through the wire, with infantry following and the attack began early in the morning of 20 November 1917."

He is listed on the Roll of Honour for Croydon, but again any details about him are few and far between.

• •

This photograph of Dawson came from the Stock Exchange Roll of Honour. He is listed on the Roll of Honour for both Croydon and the Stock Exchange, although the physical whereabouts of the latter memorial still remains a mystery.

Hugh Murray Forster

Major, King's Own Scottish Borders.

Died September 26th 1915, age 32.

Buried in Noeux-Les-Mines Communal Cemetery, Pas de Calais, France.

Forster was born in late 1883, in Newcastle-upon-Tyne, the son of Sir Ralph Collingwood Forster (1850-1930), 1st baronet of The Grange, Sutton, Surrey who had been born in Chillingham, Northumberland.

He was educated at Charterhouse School in Surrey and the Cricketarchive website shows him playing five matches for the school in 1901 and 1902. He normally batted at No.5 or No.6, although in his last recorded match, against Wellington College at Crowthorne in July 1902 he opened the batting in the second innings (having batted at No.5 in the first innings) and recorded his best score of 64. He also scored 54 the previous year against The Royal Military College, Sandhurst.

Forster did not play any first-class cricket, but was a member of Surrey from 1907-14. On September 7th 1904 he played one match for Sutton against Surrey Young Amateurs at The Oval and batting at No.3 scored 39 in his team's total of 212-9. Surrey Amateurs scored 123. On August 7th 1908 he played for the Surrey Club and Ground XI against Epsom and scored one run in a drawn match. On June 17th 1909 he played for Sutton against a Surrey Club and Ground XI and batting at No.7 failed to score. The Surrey team won by 166 runs.

Shipping records show him leaving Buenos Aires, Argentina for Southampton, England where he docked on July 12th 1913 on the Araguaya boat. He travelled first-class and his profession is shown as "Merchant".

He died at the Battle of Loos, but there is some uncertainty as to the precise date of his death, as his obituary in the 1916 *Wisden Almanack* reads: "Died in France on September 26th, of wounds received three days earlier, aged 32. He was in the Charterhouse XI in 1901 and 1902, in the former year being fourth in the averages with 34.72 and in the latter seventh with 13.25."

Of those listed on the war memorial, only Lieutenant Colonel Richard Lewis attained a higher rank. Forster, along with Burrell, is one of only two Majors.

His father was the governing director of Bessler, Waechter and Co. Merchants, Chairman of the Merchants Marine Insurance Company and Director of the Bank of Tarapaca and Argentina Limited. The family moved to The Grange, in Sutton around 1886 and his father, who was High Sheriff of Surrey in 1906, received a baronetcy in 1912. He quickly established himself as a local benefactor, donating money for the pavilion to be built at Cheam CC in Surrey, for example.

Forster's name is also on the Charterhouse School (Godalming) war memorial and he was a Freemason in the Mid Surrey Lodge (number 3109). His will shows an estate of £235 – 2s – 2d, which, for a Freemason businessman in his 30s from a wealthy family who attained the rank of Major is a surprisingly modest sum.

● ●

Sutton War Memorial, Surrey.

Forster is listed on this large war memorial at Sutton along with Hickman and Read, who are in this book. It is located in Manor Park, opposite the police station, and lists the names of 524 men who never returned from active service.

Andy Ducat, one of Surrey's biggest stars throughout his career from 1906 to 1931.

William Gerald Oliver Gill

Lieutenant, Essex Regiment.

Died March 27th 1917, age 21.

Buried in Gaza War Cemetery, Israel.

Gill was born on May 26th 1895 near Norwood, London, the son of William and Louisa, of "St. Ives," Chatsworth Road, West Norwood, London. He was baptised on July 22nd 1895 in Holy Trinity Church, Tulse Hill, London.

Gill was educated at Dulwich College, in southeast London, where excellent records about him have been maintained. He played for the College first XI in 1913, and in the same year for both the rugby first XV and first VI Gymnasium. He played cricket for Dulwich College three times in 1913; against Bedford Grammar School (batting at No.3 he scored 11 runs but he did not bat in the second innings), against Brighton College (at No.3 he scored three runs in a single innings match) and against St Paul's School, Kensington, London (at No.3 failed to score in his only innings and took one wicket in the opposition's only innings which saw St Paul's win easily on first innings scores).

He did not play any first-class cricket, but did turn out for Surrey Young Amateurs without any great success five times at The Oval in late 1913, each time batting down the order. On August 18th and 19th against Young Professionals of Surrey he scored 11 and one as his team lost by 16 runs, on the 20th against Young Amateurs of Essex he scored seven as his team won by 268 runs, on the 21st against Young Amateurs of Middlesex he scored one as his team won by 325 runs, on the 22nd against Gentlemen of Surrey he scored 14* as his team won by one wicket and lastly, on September 3rd against Wanderers he scored one in his team's total of 191 as they lost by two wickets. In the Wanderers' team were Francis Gillespie, Frank Nightingale and Thomas Stafford who were killed in action and who all feature in this book. In none of these matches did Gill bowl.

In January 1914 Gill went with a private tutor to Germany to learn the language and visit all parts of the country. On his return in May 1914 he was articled to Slater & Co, Chartered Accountants.

Gill's death was mentioned in *The Times* on April 12th 1917 and below the report is a photograph of him in military uniform. The report states: "He was a keen and all-round athlete and secured his 'colours' for cricket, for Rugby football, and as a member of the first six (gymnasium). He played for the Young Amateurs of Surrey at the Oval in 1913 and for Dulwich Cricket Club during part of 1914. He had only started his business career a few weeks when the war broke out, and he then joined the Inns of Court OTC (Officer Training

Corps)... He went abroad with his regiment in March, 1916."

The school's Roll of Honour records: "In March 1915, he took a commission in the Essex Regiment (T.F.) and was attached to the 2/7th Battalion in England. In March 1916 he proceeded to Egypt to join his own battalion, the 1/5th, and was present at the battle of Rumani in August. The advance into Palestine was started in January following, and he was with his regiment at the first battle of Gaza, being killed whilst attacking the Turkish trenches on Ali Munter Hill on 27th March 1917. Though good at all his games, it was not only as a sportsman that he made his mark, his straightforward, open character, unselfishness, and high-spirited humorous disposition enabled him to brighten many an hour among those with whom he came into contact – not only at School but in his Army career too."

His obituary in the 1918 *Wisden Almanack* reads: "Killed, March 27, aged 21. Dulwich College XI, 1913, when, with 113 as his best score, he had an average of 36, coming out fourth for a strong side. Left-handed bat with a good defence, a good field. Played for Young Amateurs of Surrey in 1913."

In a touching letter from his father William in response to a request from Dulwich College for more information about his son for inclusion in their Roll of Honour, he writes: "I really feel very much ashamed of myself for neglecting to reply to your former official communication. The fact is I shirk diving into matters connected with our dear boy who is gone & opening up wounds which, though I am not morbid, probably never will be far below the surface. Gerald was a singular mixture. Very keen on Sports & painstaking to excel in them, yet with a disposition more like a lovable girl's than a sporting youth's. He was full of the joy of life in its most active forms, yet a thinker and a great reader & writer. His active

Army life had made no difference to this serious trait in his character apparently from his writings home and the fact that the book he was reading on his last march into Palestine was HG Wells' classic *An Englishman Looks at the World*".

His name is on the war memorial affixed to the front of St Luke's Church, West Norwood, London and also the war memorial at his old school.

• •

This clear photograph of Gill is to be found below a good length obituary for him which featured in *The Times* on April 12th 1917.

Extracts from

The Times

Thursday, April 12, 1917.

KILLED IN ACTION.

GILL.—Killed in action, on the 27th March, 1917, WILLIAM GERALD OLIVER GILL, 2nd Lieutenant, Essex Regiment, elder beloved son of Mr. and Mrs. William W. Gill, of Norwood, aged 21. In proud and loving memory.

SECOND LIEUTENANT WILLIAM GERALD OLIVER GILL, Essex Regiment, killed on March 27, aged 21, was the elder son of Mr. and Mrs. William W. Gill, of Norwood, and a grandson of the late Mr. George Conquest. He was educated at Dulwich College, where he was selected for a house scholarship. He was a keen and all-round athlete and secured his " colours " for cricket, for Rugby football, and as a member of the first six (gymnasium). He played for the Young Amateurs of Surrey at the Oval in 1913, and for the Dulwich Cricket Club during part of 1914. He had only started his business career a few weeks when the war broke out, and he then joined the Inns of Court O.T.C. While in a reserve battalion of the Essex Regiment he commanded a company with the temporary rank of lieutenant. He went abroad with his regiment in March, 1916.

A number of those featured in this book had very short obituaries in *The Times*, normally just a few lines under a subtitle of "Killed in Action", but Gill is unusual as he has a more detailed obituary which covers his family, education, sporting achievements and military career.

St Luke's Church, West Norwood, London.

Gill is listed on a large war memorial affixed to the outside of this church which is very close to the local High Street and railway station. His name is the fourth one down in the right column.

Cyril Wilkinson – Surrey CCC Captain 1914-1920.

Francis Sydney Gillespie

Captain, Royal Sussex Regiment.

Died June 18th 1916, age 26.

Buried in Merville Community Cemetery, Nord, France.

Gillespie was born on March 26th 1889 in Croydon, Surrey, the son of John and Eleanor, of 102 West Hill, Sydenham, Kent. He was educated at Dulwich College and whilst there played cricket for the second XI in 1904.

He played for WG Grace's London County XI, whose home ground was at the local Crystal Palace Park, as well as Surrey Club and Ground in 1911 and 1912, Gentlemen of Surrey between 1911 and 1914, Surrey second XI and six matches for the Surrey first-team in 1913. He was also a member of the club between 1912 and 1914.

In his six first-class appearances he scored 249 runs at 22.63, with a top score of 72 being his only contribution over 50. He also held two catches. On August 28th 1914 he played for Wanderers against Young Amateurs of Surrey at The Oval and opened the batting, scoring 37 and eight as his side won by 13 runs.

There are copious reports about him in the school's Roll of Honour including this entry which states: "He was a left-handed batsman, but unfortunately had not the time to devote to county cricket. Subsequently he joined his father's firm in the City, and was only able to play club cricket, being a member of the Wanderers, for which club he made his record score of 217 not out in 1912. Within a week of the outbreak of war he joined the Honourable Artillery Company and shortly afterwards obtained a temporary commission in the 13th Service Battalion Sussex Regiment. He went through the Hythe School of Musketry with 200 others and passed out top with a certificate of distinction. In July 1915, he was promoted temporary Captain and in March 1916, went out to France. He was badly wounded while out in 'no man's land', only a few yards from the Germans' wire entanglement, on patrol work near Ypres, and died some hours afterwards on 18th June 1916, greatly missed by everyone. He was buried at Merville."

His obituary in the 1917 *Wisden Almanack* reads: "Died of wounds on June 18. He was not in the XI while at Dulwich but afterwards played with success for London County, Surrey and the Wanderers. He was a left-handed batsman and in 1912 and 1913 headed the Surrey 2nd XI averages; in the former year he made 105 v Wiltshire at The Oval, and in the latter 57 and 55 not out v Glamorgan on the same ground. Tried for Surrey in 1913, he made 249 runs with an average of 22.62, his highest score being 72 against Gloucestershire at The Oval."

His school still have a letter, signed by GA Gillespie of "Hollow Combe, West Hill, Sydenham, SE 26" which outlines some details about him and his death, alongside a photograph.

The Surrey CCC yearbooks show that he played for Gentlemen of Surrey against the 2nd battalion of the Honourable Artillery Company (HAC) at The Oval on July 31st 1915. He failed to score in his team's total of 312, but they comfortably beat the HAC who only realised 132.

Another lengthy obituary from an unknown newspaper which was passed to me by his school, states that after a few appearances for the Surrey XI "he joined his father's firm, John Gillespie and Co., 2 Whittington-avenue, EC. Within a week of the outbreak of war he joined the HAC and shortly afterwards obtained a commission… the battalion has lost an officer whom it can ill afford to spare at this time. His first thought was always for his men. He studied their interests, and his relations with them were of the happiest. They feel his loss very much indeed, and I know that when the time comes they will avenge it."

The Norwood News produced a "Roll of Honour" devoting a full page to Gillespie with an accompanying photograph. The opening three paragraphs feature two letters from army colleagues to his parents about the loss of their son and afterwards the article remarks: "Captain Gillespie will probably be remembered best by the world of cricket as 'Bobby' Gillespie. Born 26 years ago, he was educated at Dulwich College, where he learnt his cricket, but it was with the London County Club at the Crystal Palace, with the great 'WG' as manager and captain, that he developed the cricket powers which ultimately led him into the Surrey County team… Thus one more gallant and capable young officer has gone; the parents mourn the loss of a brave, dutiful and loving son, and a large number of personal friends will sadly miss

the genial, manly and honest friendship of a true type of gallant gentleman."

••

This clear photograph of Gillespie comes from the detailed records that his old school, Dulwich College, have commendably kept on many of their ex-pupils. It was next to his obituary in a long and detailed write-up in their Roll of Honour, which the school produced to commemorate their ex-pupils who were killed in action in the Great War.

Merville Community Cemetery, Nord, France.

Gillespie is buried in a village which saw fighting between the Germans and French and British cavalry early in October 1914. The area was a railhead until May 1915 and a hospital centre from 1915-18. The cemetery was used by French troops in October 1914, and for Commonwealth burials from then until March 1918. It contains 1,268 Great War Commonwealth burials and 12 French war graves.

Reginald Nigel Gipps

Lieutenant, Scots Guards.

Died November 7th 1914, age 23.

Listed on the Menin Gate Memorial, Ypres, West Vlaanderen, Belgium.

Gipps was born on November 22nd 1891, near Hanover Square in central London, the son of General Sir Reginald Gipps GCB of Sycamore House, Farnborough, Hampshire. His father had been commissioned into the Scots Guards in 1849 and fought in the Crimean War. At the battle of Alma he received a bayonet wound and was made Commanding Officer of the battalion in 1874.

Gipps junior was a schoolboy member of the club from 1909-11 and a full member from 1912-13 although it appears that he did not play any cricket of a noteworthy level. He was also a member of the Guards' and Boodle's clubs.

He was educated at Wellington College, Crowthorne, Berkshire and The Royal Military College at Sandhurst and was gazetted Second Lieutenant Scots Guards on February 4th 1911. He was promoted to Lieutenant on January 19th 1913. He served in Egypt and later with the Expeditionary Force in France and Flanders and died near Ypres. His body was never identified, so he is listed with over 54,000 others on the huge Menin Gate Memorial in Ypres, Belgium.

The CWGC website states: "The site of the Menin Gate was chosen because of the hundreds of thousands of men who passed through it on their way to the battlefields. It commemorates those of all Commonwealth nations, except New Zealand, who died in the Salient, in the case of United Kingdom casualties before 16 August 1917 (with some exceptions)... bears the names of more than 54,000 officers and men whose graves are not known."

An extract from the War Diary of the First Battalion, Scots Guards says: "The 4th (November 1914) was a comparatively quiet day, on which a point d'appui [an assembly point] was made at a burnt farm-house near Gheluvelt. In this position the line remained till the 7th, suffering from German artillery fire on each day. On the 4th and 5th reinforcements of 110 men arrived, and Lieutenants RN Gipps and FA Monckton were killed on the 7th."

Inside the Victoria Road cemetery chapel in Farnborough, Hampshire, is an ornate memorial to Gipps.

His will shows two addresses; 29 and 30 St James's Street, Middlesex and 26 and 27 Bury Street, Middlesex and an enormous estate of £77,930 – 19s – 2d. The executor was Robert Basil Feilden who had been a Captain in the Royal Artillery.

This photograph was found on a website called Oldwhitelodge.com. Dedicated to the "History of The Sycamores and Old White Lodge" it records "the history of the two houses and their occupants from the 1860s though to the present day. It's a story that spans the Crimean, Boer and Great War. It shows how the Great War destroyed the lives of three generations of the families that lived in the house.

Victoria Road Chapel, Farnborough, Hampshire.

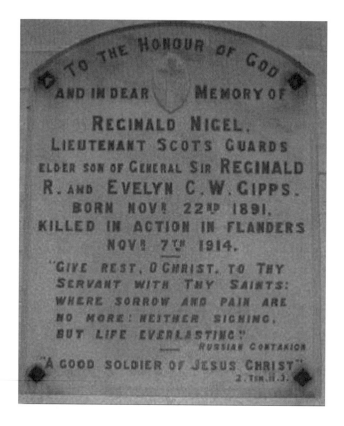

Gipps is commemorated by way of this large plaque in a chapel in Farnborough, Hampshire. This photograph was also found on the website Oldwhitelodge.com along with two photographs of him in a suit; one in the company of his sister Evelyn and the other alone.

C. Green

Rank and regiment not known.

Died – not known.

Place of burial not known.

Green is the problem name on the war memorial, and Surrey's very own Unknown Soldier. According to the CWGC records there were 164 men named C Green killed in the Great War. Distinguishing our C Green from so many others proved difficult. Had his rank been shown on the memorial we would have at least been able to eliminate a number of possibilities, but no such luck.

The individual records for these 164 casualties named C Green vary between detailed and very brief. After viewing individual records that contained detailed domestic information, it was possible to discount many, but this increases the chance that our casualty is one of those about whom the CWGC knows very little, or nothing, bar their name.

What we can establish is that neither the Surrey first XI, nor any lesser county XI has ever contained a player called C Green, so, given the criteria for inclusion on the memorial board, our casualty will most likely have been a member of the club, or employed by the club in some capacity. Pursuing this line of enquiry, a check through old Surrey CCC yearbooks provides three instances of a member with this surname who were worth exploring.

Charles Green, a schoolboy member from 1908-14.

CE Green, a full member from 1885-1914.

CT Green, a full member from 1886-87.

Charles Green. The 1923 yearbook shows the year that each member first joined the club and a Charles Green did so in 1919 after the end of hostilities. Perhaps he was the schoolboy member from 1908-14, now old enough to be a full member? If this fact could be established, then he can be ignored as a possible candidate, as he survived the war.

That scenario aside, there are 127 casualties killed in the Great War who are recorded with Charles as a first or middle name and Green as a surname.

CE Green. If the CE Green from the yearbooks, the full member from 1885-1914, became a full member on reaching the age of 19, as some others did, then at the start of the Great War he would have been at least 48, and therefore highly unlikely to have joined up. It's possible that he began his membership as a junior in 1885, but the schoolboy (junior) and full members were listed together in the yearbooks before 1904; younger members have "jun" after their names. CE Green does not have this after his name in any of the yearbooks in which he is listed as a member.

Although there are 11 casualties recorded as CE Green – and we have ages and details for some – the vast majority can be ignored due to their location or age:

1. Private in Oxford and Bucks Light Infantry, lived in Bucks – aged 21.

2. Corporal in Queen's Own West Kent Regiment, lived in Rusthall near Tunbridge Wells – aged 38.

3. Private in Canadian Mounted Rifles Battalion, a Canadian.

4. Second Lieutenant in London Regiment, lived in North Woolwich, London.

5. Private in Leicestershire Regiment, lived in Leicestershire – aged 22.

6. Private in Middlesex Regiment, lived in Hendon, London – aged 35.

7. Lance Corporal in Argyll and Sutherland Highlanders, lived in Edinburgh, Scotland – aged 20.

8. Private in Machine Gun Corps, lived in Peckham, London.

9. Second Lieutenant in King's Shropshire Light Infantry.

10. Lance Corporal in Hampshire Regiment, lived in Southampton.

11. A Saddler in Essex Yeomanry.

Having conducted further enquiries with military enthusiasts and by applying a degree of common sense, numbers four, six and eight in this list seem the best candidates to be our casualty.

Number four is Cecil Ernest Green, who went to France on December 13th 1916. He was commissioned as a Second Lieutenant into the London Regiment on April 24th 1918 and his widow lived in Norbury.

Number six is Charles Edward Green, a Private in the Middlesex Regiment, who played for Millwall FC and was a tram-cleaner in Finchley, North London. The football club only knows his occupation and little else.

Number eight is another Charles Edward Green, a Private in the Machine Gun Corps, who was born and lived in Peckham. He enlisted at Camberwell and eventually joined the Machine Gun Corps, via the Royal Berkshire Regiment. He was posted to France on August 25th 1916.

CT Green. If CT Green had first been a full member in 1886 then even if, like Harold Noakes, he joined as young as nine, he would have been aged between 36 and 40 during the war, a perfectly plausible fighting age. In the CWGC's records there are ten CT Greens shown as killed in the Great War.

There are reasonable domestic details for six of these casualties. For some there are domestic details, but they have no connections with London or Surrey; for others there are either few domestic details available, but a connection with London or Surrey, or vice versa and for some there are few domestic details and no connection with either area.

Amongst them is a Charles Taylor Green, a Second Lieutenant in the Royal West Surrey Regiment and a Charles Thomas Green, a

Private in the Royal Fusiliers, from North Woolwich, London. Both were 19 when killed so could not have been a full member as far back as 1886-87, and therefore should probably be discounted.

Clarence Green. A search of the 164 people called C Green killed in the Great War reveals one who may have lived near to The Oval and who has no middle name. Clarence Green was a Gunner in the Royal Garrison Artillery and was born and lived in Hoxton, Middlesex. He enlisted in Stratford, Essex, died on October 1st 1915, and was the first husband of Mrs EJ Shaw (formerly Green), of 37 De Laune Street, Kennington, London (which is next to Kennington underground station, so about half-a-mile from The Oval cricket ground). However, perhaps his widow married Mr EJ Shaw and moved to Kennington with her new husband. If so, then when she was married to Clarence, they would possibly have been living elsewhere and not at this address. Whilst a residence near Kennington is rare for most of the other casualties, he is a C Green, so is a good candidate.

Candidates

So we have four casualties with a surname of Green and one initial of C who remain good candidates for our Unknown Soldier;

a. Cecil Ernest Green, a Second Lieutenant in the London Regiment.

b. Charles Edward Green, a Private in the Middlesex Regiment.

c. Charles Edward Green, a Private in the Machine Gun Corps.

d. Clarence Green, a Gunner in the Royal Garrison Artillery.

With the exception of JH Hunt, the initials of those on the war memorial tally exactly with the details about casualties held by the CWGC. If our casualty was a CE Green, would he not be listed on the war memorial as such?

Conclusion

So where does that leave us? Is our man one of the 164 C. Greens about which the CWGC know little? Is he Clarence Green whose wife lived tantalisingly close to The Oval but wasn't a member of Surrey? Could it even have been an error, and did C Green return from the war after all to become the member of Surrey who joined in 1919? Whoever he was, C Green is emblematic of a conflict that destroyed so many lives, some of which have left but the faintest trace. At the risk of him becoming my "white whale", I fancy there is more work to be done if we are to afford him the memory his sacrifice deserves.

••

Tomb Of The Unknown Warrior.

Arthur Kendrick Hickman

Lieutenant, Royal Welsh Fusiliers.

Died April 5th 1916, age 23.

Listed on the Basra War Memorial, Iraq.

Hickman was born on July 28th 1892 in Epsom, Surrey, the son of Arthur and Mary of "L'Ancresse", Egmont Road, Sutton, Surrey. He had five siblings – Ruby, Mary, Enid, Gordon and Joan.

He was educated at Clifton College, Bristol from 1906, going up to Trinity College, Oxford in 1911 where he spent one year before entering the London Stock Exchange. He was a schoolboy member of Surrey from 1910-11 and a full member from 1912-14.

He played for Surrey Young Amateurs from 1909-11 and again in 1914. On June 24th 1913 he played for Gentlemen of Surrey against Epsom College at Epsom and opened the batting, but is shown "retired ill" with a score of 47 in a total of 304 in reply to the Epsom total of 85.

I am indebted to Hickman's great-nephew, Richard Pollard, the grandson of Arthur's sister Ruby, who sent me letters from the front (see Appendix 2) as well as details of Hickman's active service career in which he writes: "[Arthur] first saw action in Flanders in October 1914 and later fought in the trenches in France. He returned to England in March 1915 to become an officer (lieutenant) with the Royal Welsh Fusiliers. He

was then sent to Gallipoli and took part in the evacuation of Suvla Bay and Helles in December 1915. Thereafter he was stationed in Egypt from where he was sent to Mesopotamia to take part in the relief of Kut. British and Indian forces under General Townshend had taken Kut but were subsequently trapped and under siege from the Turks. Arthur was part of a force of around 30,000 troops to make a final attempt to break through the Turkish lines. The attack began on April 4th and on the following day a Turkish position at Al Hannah was captured. A decision was made to advance to the next Turkish position at Falahiyah and this began on the afternoon of April 5th. It was there that Arthur was killed leading his platoon. He was shot in the neck and died immediately. He was buried the next day, in full uniform where he fell. The grave was deliberately unmarked in order to avoid being desecrated by the 'Arabs', as one letter from Colonel Hay explains. The grave is located 700-800 yards from the River Tigris, on the left (north) bank near the Falahiyah position."

Falahiyah was eventually captured but the relief of Kut was ultimately unsuccessful. In one of the most shameful incidents of the war, it later transpired that General Townshend had lied about his predicament at Kut in an attempt to speed up the relief operation. He surrendered on April 29th but negotiated his own safe passage to an island off the coast of Istanbul where he is said to have been attended by two officers, two orderlies, an Indian servant and a Portuguese cook. Meanwhile he abandoned his troops, most of whom died in forced marches or in Turkish prison camps. In total, around 23,000 Commonwealth troops are estimated to have died in the failed relief of Kut; 2,000 on the same day as Hickman.

His obituary in the 1917 *Wisden Almanack* reads: "Killed in action on April 4 or 5, aged 23, was in the Clifton XI in 1909 and two following seasons. In 1911 when he was second in the averages with 38.30, he scored 29 and 157 not out v. Rugby, and 37 and 30 v. Cheltenham." Inside the school sports pavilion is a photograph of him in the 1911 Clifton School cricket team.

As his grave is not marked, he is listed on the Basra War Memorial in Iraq and CWGC records state: "Until 1997 the Basra Memorial was located on the main quay of the naval dockyard at Maqil on the west bank of the Shatt-al-Arab, about 8 kilometres north of Basra. Because of the sensitivity of the site, the Memorial was moved by presidential decree. The move, carried out by the authorities in Iraq, involved a considerable amount of manpower, transport costs and sheer engineering on their part, and the Memorial has been re-erected in its entirety. The Basra Memorial is now located 32 kilometres along the road to Nasiriyah, in the middle of what was a major battleground during the first Gulf War."

Hickman is listed on the war memorial at Sutton, Surrey and there is a plaque to his memory in All Saint's Church, All Saint's Road, Sutton. His name can also be found on the very weathered war memorial in the churchyard as well as a memorial to his memory inside Llanwnog Church in Wales which reads: "In Loving Memory of ARTHUR KENDRICK HICKMAN, Lieut RWF, eldest and dearly loved son of ARTHUR and

MARY HICKMAN. Born July 28th 1892, killed in action April 5th 1916, while bravely leading his men in an effort to relieve Kut. RIP".

•••••••••••••••••••••••••••••••••••••

Hickman in full military dress. I'm particularly taken by his somewhat haunted expression.

Trinity College, Oxford XI, 1912.

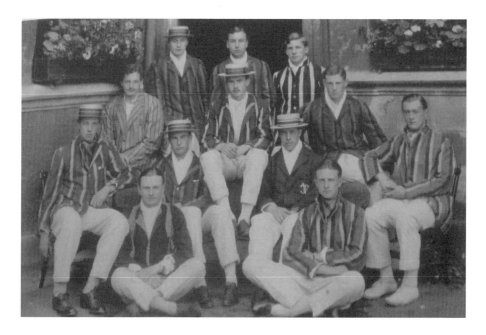

Hickman can be seen standing in the centre of the back row in this clear photograph of the Trinity College, Oxford XI from 1912.

Sutton War Memorial, Surrey.

Hickman is listed on this large suburban war memorial along with Forster and Read. He is one of a few to be listed on multiple memorials; in his case a large plaque inside a local church.

Ernie Hayes, a star all-rounder for Surrey in the years leading up to the Great War.

Charles Morgan Hoare

Lieutenant, 15th (The Kings) Hussars.

Died August 24th 1914, age 21.

Listed on the La-Ferte-Sous-Jouarre Memorial, Seine-et-Marne, France.

Hoare was born in early 1893 in Chelsea, London, the son of Charles Twysden Hoare, of Bignell Park, Bicester, Oxfordshire. The 1901 census shows him aged eight and living in the Baltonborough area of Wells, Somerset with his mother, Blanche. Come the 1911 census he is a boarding student at The Royal Agricultural College in Cirencester, Gloucestershire.

He was educated at Osborne and Dartmouth, with the intention of him joining the Royal Navy, but he elected to join the Army. He is mentioned in the *London Gazette* on January 5th 1912 "to be Second Lieutenant. Dated 24th October 1911." and is shown as being in the Queen's Own, Oxfordshire Hussars. He features again in the *London Gazette* on January 9th 1914 as "Second Lieutenant (on probation) to be Second Lieutenant. Dated 24th December 1913." This time, he is shown as being in the 15th (The Kings) Hussars. The first entry made no mention of him being made Second Lieutenant on probation however and there is a gap of over two years between entries.

Although he did not play any first-class cricket, or at any noticeable level, he was a member of the club from 1912-14. He was fond of polo, hunting and point to point racing and a member of the Carlton Club in St James' in central London.

He is mentioned in the History of the 15th The King's Hussars (1914-22), which tells that he "left England in August with the British Expeditionary Force and his troops went to Havre", and that "he soon met the enemy and only extricated himself by hard fighting, falling back to the village of St Symphorien, from which he was summarily ejected." The history carries on to say that the squadron galloped the village (i.e. charged it, but with no specific objective) and after gaining it with no opposition continued to the village of Blangies. Their maps were inaccurate, so the squadron formed columns of fours and proceeded down the main street, swords drawn. A little way in they encountered a barricade and had no room to deploy due to the garden walls and houses alongside. The enemy then opened up with machine guns and the squadron was virtually wiped out. Later the book reveals that Hoare "fell at the head of his men."

He was the first person on the war memorial to be killed in action, in his case just 20 days after England had declared war on Germany. His grave is not marked, so, like Charles Sills who was killed 33 days later, he is listed on one of the memorials to those with no known grave.

The memorial is located about 43 miles east of Paris and the CWGC records say that it "commemorates nearly 4,000 officers and men of the British Expeditionary Force who died in August, September and the early part of October 1914 and who have no known grave."

His father, Charles Twysden Hoare (1851-1935) played first-class cricket for an England XI, Gentlemen of England, MCC, Middlesex, the South and Surrey (in 1871 and 1874) and for many other clubs which included Eastbourne, Eton Ramblers, Gentlemen of England, Gentlemen of Sussex, Gentlemen of West Kent, Harlequins, Hastings, I Zingari, and Oxford University.

Hoare's name is on the Roll of Honour at West Downs School in Winchester, Hampshire, the war memorial in the foyer of St Edburg's Church in Bicester and also on the war memorial in St Mary's Church, Chesterton, Oxfordshire.

....

St Mary's Church, Chesterton, Oxfordshire.

Hoare's name, rank and regiment are on this colourful war memorial, set back in an old door opening. The village church was re-built in the 13th century and re-consecrated in 1238. Although born in London, his father had connections with Bignell Park, which is close to the church, so this may have been where he worshipped.

St Edburg's Church, Bicester, Oxfordshire.

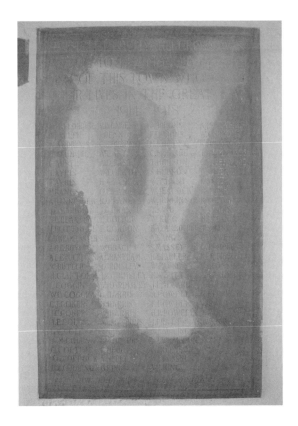

Hoare is also commemorated on this badly stained war memorial to those who fell in the Great War which is located in the church porch. He is thus listed on three memorials; inside and outside of two Oxfordshire churches and on the one at his old school in Hampshire.

Bernard Henry Holloway

Captain, Royal Sussex Regiment.

Died September 27th 1915, age 27.

Listed on the Loos Memorial, Pas de Calais, France.

Holloway was born on January 13th 1888, near Wandsworth Common, Surrey, the son of Sir Henry and Lady Holloway of Draxmont, Wimbledon Hill, Wimbledon, Surrey.

He was educated at Ley's School in Cambridge and later at Jesus College Cambridge (along with his three younger brothers) and played for the school cricket XI from 1904-07, proving himself to be a fine all-rounder as well as captain. He was third in the batting averages in 1904, second in 1905 and 1906 and top in 1907. Although he did not gain a blue when at Cambridge, he did play in the trial matches in 1911.

Whilst still at school he played for Surrey Club and Ground in 1906 and on leaving school, again in 1908. He was selected for Young Amateurs in 1906 and 1907, Gentlemen of Surrey in June 1908 and for Wanderers in both 1908 and 1909. During 1910-11 he went to the West Indies with an MCC team and scored 443 runs at 24.61 which included a century against British Guiana at Georgetown. Between 1910 and 1914 he played 11 matches for MCC and eight matches for Sussex between 1911 and 1914, for whom he scored 232 runs. On August 28th 1914 he played for Wanderers

against Young Amateurs of Surrey at The Oval, scoring 17 and taking 5-39 and 6-20 opening the bowling as his side won by 13 runs.

He played rugby for Cambridge v Oxford in 1907 and again in 1909, formerly at at half back and latterly at three-quarter back. In the 1909 match he was stunned early in the match and, being a lifelong teetotaller, apparently he imagined the sensation must have been comparable to being drunk. He was also in the university lacrosse team from 1908-10, captaining the side in 1910, the year he appeared for England.

Holloway has a good length obituary in *Wisden Almanack* and is commemorated on a website for Jesus College, Cambridge in which many curious biographical details are recorded. He was known as 'Babe', mainly because of "a complexion which would have created the reputation of any face cream on the market". Jesus College's website goes on to say: "He narrowly missed a blue for cricket, where he was a dashing batsman. He was a sociable man and was a member of the College societies, in spite of preferring 'ginger beer to the more heady wines.' It seems that his refusal to drink or smoke caused some puzzlement to his fellow students and the fact that he stuck with the teetotalism to the end of his life was noted in his obituary. He was obviously outspoken about his political views as it was felt that he 'would be an asset to any dinner table outside the Carlton Club'", from which we can conclude his sympathies did not lie with the Conservatives.

His body was never identified so he is remembered on the Loos Memorial.

His brother Norman (1889-1964) gained a blue for cricket at Cambridge and played 25 matches for the University as well as 67 for Sussex.

Before the 2014 Varsity rugby match at Twickenham, Holloway was memorialised in a wreath laying ceremony to mark the deaths of the 55 "Blues" who died in the Great War. Laying the wreath and representing The Leys School, which lost a staggering 149 former pupils during the conflict, was their headmaster, Martin Priestley.

Holloway's will shows an address of Burntwood Grange, Upper Tooting, Surrey, his executor as Henry, Roland and Herbert Holloway, builders and a massive estate of £10,540 – 11s – 6d. Clearly his temperance was not driven by enforced thrift.

....

Bernard and Norman are shown here in the Natives Annual photo call (a tradition that still continues). Norman is front row extreme right and Bernard is immediately to his right. Thanks to the Natives for permission to use this photograph.

The County Ground, Hove, Sussex.

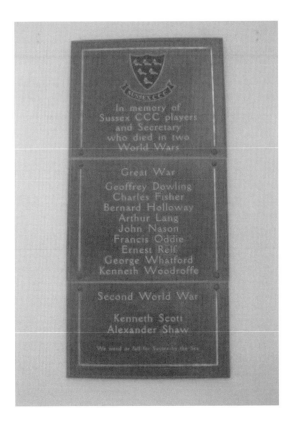

Holloway is also memorialised on the Sussex CCC war memorial at Hove, erected in 2014.

John Howell

Lieutenant, 15th (The Kings) Hussars.

Died September 25th 1915, age 20.

Listed on the Menin Gate Memorial, Ypres, West Vlaanderen, Belgium.

Howell was born on July 5th 1895 in Thames Ditton, Surrey, the son of Reg and Nona of Clive House, Esher, Surrey.

He was educated at Repton School in Derbyshire between 1908 and 1914 where he played cricket from 1911-14 (captain 1914), football 1911-13 (captain 1913) and was Head Prefect in 1913. Thankfully Repton have kept good records and details about him and he is well commemorated at the school. He came to Repton from Sandroyd School, near Salisbury.

He was a schoolboy member of Surrey from 1908-14 and although he did not play first-class cricket, he played for Surrey Young Amateurs in 1913 and 1914, Surrey second XI in 1913 and for Public Schools, Repton and a couple of matches for The Rest against Lord's Schools at Lord's in 1913 and 1914. His last recorded match on the Cricketarchive website was a two-day match for Public Schools against MCC at Lord's, which began on August 5th 1914 and saw him score 28 opening the batting. His brother Miles opened the batting for MCC and scored 26 in a low-scoring drawn match. Miles also went to Repton and later captained Oxford University at cricket and football as well as playing 36 matches for Surrey between 1919

and 1925. Reginald, his father, played three matches for Surrey between 1878 and 1889 and died at Esher in Surrey in 1912.

Howell enlisted as a Private in the Artist's Rifles in August 1914 and by December had progressed to Second Lieutenant in the 9th King's Royal Rifle Corps. Like his brother Miles, he had no leaning towards a life in the military, but out of a sense of duty took a commission. Miles, who died in February 1976, was wounded in the Dardenelles and John appears to have been killed on his first day in action, in a failed attack on Bellewarde Farm at Hooge in Belgium.

His burial plot is not marked so, like Curwen and Gipps, he is listed on the impressive Menin Gate Memorial at Ypres with over 54,000 others who lie in unmarked graves.

In *Repton Cricket* (1901-51) by FR D'O Monro (1953) is the following passage about Howell, written by Alfred Cochrane: "It is doubtful if we have ever had a better batsman at Repton than John Howell was during the last two seasons. Crawford and Francis Ford were more powerful and brilliant, but they were not more difficult to get out. Fry and Lionel Palairet were at their best some years after they left school; and of that company of fine men who, a few seasons ago, won matches under Altham's captaincy there was not one who individually could compare with Howell as he was in 1913 and 1914. Long innings were characteristic of him. Many more boys can play a good innings than can play a long innings, indeed the same can be said of many men. Howell could go on hour after hour batting with a machine-like accuracy of a first-rate professional. Such proficiency requires certain qualities of concentration, as well as the power to recognise your own limitations. The neatness of Howell's style made him always worth watching, while the variety of his strokes and his admirable onside play made him anything but a slow scorer. When he was in form it looked hopeless to bowl to him, and no player of his years gave his innings away less often."

There is a photograph of him in the cricket pavilion at Repton School going out to bat with Jack Hobbs and at the school is the John Howell Room where the cricket teams have lunch and tea. The John Howell bat is still awarded to the best player each year.

The *Wisden Almanack* obituary for George William Edendale Whitehead, killed on October 17th 1915 states: "Among the many public school cricketers lost during the war perhaps none, except John Howell of Repton, had better prospects of winning distinction at the game than George Whitehead…"

The comprehensive obituary of Howell himself in *Wisden Almanack* records: "Howell was killed in Flanders on September 25. Among all the young cricketers who have fallen in the War not one of brighter promise than John Howell can be named. Judging from his wonderful record at Repton it is not too much to say that he was potentially an England batsman. But for the War he would have been at Oxford last year and would no doubt have been seen in the Surrey XI at The Oval. Born on the 5th of July, 1895,

he was only twenty when he lost his life. He was in the Repton team for four seasons -- 1911 to 1914 -- being captain in 1914. From the first he showed great promise as a batsman, his style having obviously been modelled on that of Tom Hayward. He did well in 1911 and 1912, and in the next two years he was probably the best school bat in England. In 1913 he scored 737 runs for Repton, with an average of 56, and in 1914, 686 runs with an average of 52. He took some little time to find his form in school cricket in 1914, but he scored 202 not out against the Old Reptonians and 202 against Uppingham. In a trial match at the Oval at the beginning of the season he played an innings of 109. In 1913 he scored 108 and 114 against the Old Reptonians, and 144 for Young Surrey Amateurs against Young Essex Amateurs. Towards the close of the season in 1913 he journeyed up to Walsall with Surrey's Second XI for the express purpose of playing against Barnes's bowling and had the satisfaction of scoring 45."

Although Howell's name is still well-known and well-publicised at Repton where he was educated, the school is also to be commended on keeping so many photographs of him.

This is one of the five of him in cricket attire that Repton School sent me and it shows him in a relaxed, if slightly portentous mode wearing a blazer and cricket whites in a team photograph.

Esher War Memorial, Surrey.

Howell is listed on this war memorial, close to where his parents lived. The inscription reads: "Those whom this cross commemorates were numbered among the men who at the call of King and Country left all that was dear to them, endured hardness, faced danger and finally passed out of the sight of men by the path of duty and self-sacrifice, giving up their own lives that others might live in freedom. Let those who come after see to it that their names be not forgotten."

Frank Lewis Hunt

Quarter Master Sergeant, Royal Field Artillery.

Died May 16th 1918, age 37.

Buried in Mikra British Cemetery, Kalamaria, Greece.

Hunt was born in early 1880 in Camberwell, London, which is about a mile from The Oval, the son of John, a leather merchant, and Emily of Tooting Graveney, London. He was baptised at St James' Church, Camberwell, London on January 18th 1880 by the vicar, Mr Dyke.

He married Helene Lucas on June 19th 1907 at St Alban's Church, Streatham Park, London and his profession is shown as an architect and surveyor. The 1911 census shows him and his wife living at 34 Half Moon Lane, Herne Hill, London with the family of his brother Edwin and his profession as "Architect". Two servants are also shown living at the address.

The yearbooks show that he was a member of the club from 1901-13 and also on the Surrey Committee in 1912. He did not play any first-class cricket, but did get selected for the Surrey Colts in 1901 and for the Club and Ground XI 1901-02, 1904-07 and in 1909 as a tail-end batsman and bowler. He also played for Merton against the Young Amateurs in September 1900.

There are 160 F Hunts shown in the CWGC records as falling in the Great War, but only four are shown as FL Hunt all having the first name of Frank. One of the four had connections with

Tooting, one with Canada and the other two hailed from Australia. The final part of the jigsaw came from a Great War enthusiast who supplied details from the National Probate Service which showed a Frank Lewis Hunt from Tooting dying in Salonica on May 16th 1918.

CWGC records show the address of his widow, Helene, as 545 Lordship Lane, East Dulwich, London although his will shows an address of 22 Chillerton Road, Tooting, Surrey.

The medal index card for Hunt shows him to be a Quarter Master Sergeant in the Royal Artillery and that he served in Eygpt and the Balkans. It also shows that like many other casualties in this war, he was awarded the 1915 Star, the British Medal and the Victory Medal. Or Pip, Squeak and Wilfred as they were often called.

Hunt was the last of those listed on the war memorial to be killed while war was still raging, although Howard Parkes died in 1920 from injuries received in action.

His name is on the war memorial at Mitcham in Surrey.

●●●●●●●●●●●●●●●●●●●●●●●●●●●●●●●●●●

Along with Stafford and Wynter, Hunt is one of three on the war memorial to be depicted in the 1911 painting of the Surrey CCC players and members which hangs in the entrance to the pavilion. On the key next to it he is number 165 and is seated at the top-right of the painting at the back.

Mitcham War Memorial, Surrey.

Hunt's name is on this war memorial, sited close to the green on which the famous Mitcham cricket team have played for over three centuries. The JH Hunt listed below him is not the casualty that follows in the book however.

Tom Hayward, one of Surrey's all-time greats whose career was prematurely ended by the outbreak of war in 1914.

John Henry Sneyd Hunt

Second Lieutenant, London Regiment.

Died September 16th 1916, age 42.

Listed on the Thiepval Memorial, Somme, France.

Hunt was born in Kensington, London on November 24th 1874 to parents Robert Ponsonby Carew Hunt and Ada Mary Hunt. He was baptised in Westminster, London on December 6th 1874. Although I have found a few errors or omissions in the ranks of casualties on the war memorial, this is the first example of a difference in the initials. However with the help of military enthusiasts and the Internet it became apparent that JHS Hunt was normally referred to as JH Hunt.

He was educated at Winchester and, according to Cricinfo, at Oxford University, although Oxford have no record of him ever having matriculated, let alone taken any exams. Curiously, he never played cricket for the school, but he did play hockey for Surrey. His late-flowering talent for cricket saw him making his highest first-class score of 128 for the Gentlemen against the Players at The Oval in 1904 in a game described by *Wisden Almanack* as "the very unsatisfactory match in which two changes were made in the Gentlemen's team after the first day." He played in the same fixture the following year and appeared in first-class cricket for Middlesex from 1902-12.

One newspaper report tells: "JH Hunt, with his big hands and huge reach, was an almost ideal fielder, and his left-handed catch in front of the pavilion which dismissed AH Hornby in the Middlesex v Lancashire match in 1905 will be remembered at Lord's". JHS Hunt played in this match batting at No.8 and opening the bowling in both innings, so we can be sure that he is the JH Hunt referred to in this short report.

His obituary in *Wisden Almanack* includes the observation that "Mr. Hunt was a very good all-round cricketer and so full of enthusiasm for the game that he was more valuable on a side than many players of greater natural gifts. He was a very plucky punishing bat, a useful change bowler – right hand fast – and a brilliant fieldsman wherever he was placed."

Hunt lived in Queen's Gardens, central London and was a clerk in the Probate and Divorce Registry. In the 1911 census he is shown as a boarder living in East Grinstead, Sussex and his occupation as "Clerk at Somerset House".

He is recorded in the Surrey yearbooks as being a member of the club from 1911-14 and on the Finance Committee in 1913 and 1914. The Committee Minute books held at the Surrey Historical Centre in Woking confirm his election to the committee in place of Stanley

Christopherson on January 16th 1913 and he is shown as J.H. Hunt. On May 21st 1914 he was elected to the Finance Committee and again also on May 20th 1915, although by this time he was in the Army.

On December 16th 1915 the committee minutes record under a title of "Letters from members of the committee" that letters were read from JH Hunt and MC Bird, although no mention is made about their contents. On May 18th 1916 the minutes show he was elected to the Cricket Committee.

His medal index card shows him enlisting as a Private on March 17th 1915 in the 15th London Regiment, gaining a Commission on July 17th 1916 with the 23rd London Regiment. He was posted as missing on September 16th 1916 which ties in well with the details obtained from the Surrey CCC Committee minutes.

On May 17th 1917 the minutes have a four-page printed notice dated April 17th 1917 attached to them, which is probably the one handed out at the Annual General Meeting. At the bottom of the front page is recorded "Messrs MC Bird, JH Hunt, AM Latham and MW Marshall retire from the Committee by rotation". By this time Hunt had been dead for seven months.

There is nothing more about him in the volume during the summer, but minutes for the meeting on November 15th 1917 record under a title of "Death of members" that "The Acting Hon. Secretary reported the following deaths of members...". JH Hunt is one of the five listed.

I was told by one military historian: "At this stage of the war, a delay of a year or so to confirm the death of a missing soldier by a Board of Inquiry was not that unusual."

Hunt is listed on the Claygate War Memorial in Surrey as JH Hunt, but the Esher Local History group when researching those listed on the memorial, show his full initials as JHS Hunt.

In his obituary in *Wisden Almanack* JHS Hunt is referred to as Mr. J.H. Hunt: "MR J H HUNT (Middlesex), born November 24, 1874, killed 1916. Details with regard to the death of Mr. Hunt have never been published. Place and date are unknown, but his friends have long given up hope that he is still alive..."

In the annual report in the 1917 yearbook, members of the first and second XIs who have been killed in action are mentioned along with JH Hunt "a member of the Committee" who we are also told "has been missing since September". *Wisden Almanack* and the Surrey yearbook both refer to him as J.H. Hunt and not JHS Hunt.

The will for JHS Hunt states: "HUNT - John Henry Sneyd of Claygate, Surrey. Second Lieutenant London Regiment died on or since 16 September 1916 in France. Probate London 12 October to Gerald Ponsonby Sneyd Hunt temporary Lieut-Colonel HM Army. Roland Cecil Sneyd Hunt Commander RN and the public trustee. Effects £7,754 – 16s – 11d."

As the above shows that he died in France and his obituary states that his death had never been publicised, I am happy that JH Hunt is the JHS Hunt listed on the Thiepval Memorial to the missing. The memorial is the biggest on The Somme and lists 72,203 names of casualties from the United Kingdom and South Africa who died in the Somme before March 20th 1918 whose final resting place is not known. Over ninety per cent of those listed on the memorial died between July and November 1916 which also fits in with the time of his death. It is located in the village of Thiepval close to the Bapaume to Albert road and was designed by Sir Edwin Lutyens. It was constructed between 1928 and 1932 and unveiled by the Prince of Wales in the presence of the President of France on August 1st 1932. There is an annual ceremony held at the memorial on July 1st, so they have not been forgotten.

His brother Lieutenant Colonel Gerald Ponsonby Sneyd Hunt of the Berkshire Regiment was killed in action on March 23rd 1918, aged 40 and is buried in Varennes Military Cemetery, which is about eight miles from Albert in France.

•••••••••••••••••••••••••••••••••••••

This photograph of Hunt in cricket attire was found on Cricinfo. It was a relief to find it so easily having spent so much time trying to prove that he was the JH Hunt on the memorial.

Claygate War Memorial, Surrey.

Hunt's name is on the village war memorial, located on the front lawn of Holy Trinity church, which is a few yards from the village green. It is interesting to note that he is listed as JH Hunt, so is recorded as such in death, much as he was in life.

Dudley Mark Hayward Jewell

Second Lieutenant, Royal Fusiliers.

Died January 20th 1916, age 22.

Buried in Guards Cemetery, Windy Corner, Cuinchy, Pas de Calais, France.

Jewell was born in early 1894 in Bexley, Kent, the fifth of six sons to Maurice and Ada, who lived at Hall Place, Bexley and previously in Chile. CWGC records show that they later lived at Warnercroft, Selsey, Sussex.

He was educated at Felsted School in Essex where he was a good all-round athlete and won his colours at cricket and football. He was a member of Worcestershire CCC when war broke out and was employed at the time in farming.

Although he did not play first-class cricket, the Cricketarchive website shows him playing two matches for his school in 1910; against Kings School, Canterbury and Leys School, Cambridge, scoring 21, 26 and 49 as an opener in three innings. He then played for Surrey Amateurs against Mitcham on September 6th and 7th 1910 at The Oval and batted at number 11 but failed to score, although he bowled three overs and returned figures of 0-34 as Mitcham won by seven wickets.

On July 31st 1911 he played for Gentlemen of Surrey against Old Johnians at Leatherhead and opened the batting with his brother Maurice, scoring 23 in a total of 237 as his team won by 143 runs. Maurice (1885-1978) who was born in Iquique, Chile played for MCC, Sussex, Worcestershire and the Surrey second XI.

Jewell joined the Royal Fusiliers on its formation in September 1914 and was gazetted to Second Lieutenant on October 27th 1914, serving with the British Expeditionary Force from November 1915.

He was killed near Givenchy whilst being employed at listening posts in the trenches. When attempting to rescue colleagues overcome by gas, he was gassed himself. His Colonel wrote to his mother saying: "I cannot tell you how much we all feel his death. He had got the most extraordinary hold over his men, and they would follow him anywhere." His Company Commander also wrote to say: "His end was most noble. He gave his life in an endeavour to save a comrade, knowing full well the risk he was taking. You must be very proud of him, just as we are."

His obituary in the 1917 *Wisden Almanack* is brief: "Killed on January 20, was in the Felsted XI in 1910 when he was second in the averages with 22.81. Subsequently he played for the Gentlemen of Surrey and Young Surrey Amateurs."

His name is on the war memorial outside St Peter's Church, Selsey in Sussex and inside the church, behind the altar, is a huge stained glass window to his memory. A short drive away is St Wilfred's chapel at Church Norton. No longer used for worship, it sits amidst a big churchyard in which there is a large white cross headstone over his mother's grave. Although not interred in the grave, Dudley is listed on the headstone with two of his brothers; Edward, who was also killed in action and Arthur, who died in 1922.

He is buried in the same cemetery as Albert Lane-Joynt, who also features in this book.

....

Jewell is commemorated in numerous places local to where his parents lived in Selsey, Sussex. This photograph was found in De Ruvigny's along with details of his short Army career.

St Peter's Church, Selsey, Sussex.

This large church window is located behind the altar. In the bottom right-hand corner is written: "To the Glory of God and in memory of Dudley Mark Hayward Jewell, Lieut. Royal Fusiliers, killed in action 20th January 1916: and of Edward Herbert Jewell, Lieut. Lancashire Fusiliers, killed in action 16th May 1916."

St Wilfred's Chapel, Church Norton, Sussex.

Jewell and his brother Edward, who was also killed in action in the Great War, are listed on the grave of their mother Ada and brother Arthur. The chapel is no longer used for regular worship, but its large graveyard remains.

Guards Cemetery, Cuinchy, Pas de Calais, France.

Jewell is one of 3,443 burials and commemorations of the First World War in this cemetery, of which 2,197 are unidentified. After The Armistice more than 2,700 graves were brought in from local battlefields such as Neuve-Chapelle, the Aubers Ridge and Festubert. The cemetery is a little west of the crossroads known to the army as "Windy Corner" where there was a house used as a dressing station and battalion headquarters.

Albert William Lane-Joynt

Lieutenant, Dorsetshire Regiment.

Died February 26th 1916, age 20.

Buried in Guards Cemetery, Windy Corner, Cuinchy, Pas de Calais, France.

Lane-Joynt was born in 1895, the son of the late Albert and Glenleigh of 32 Dover Street, London. A native of Dublin, his age is shown as eighteen in CWGC records, but further research shows him to have been aged twenty when he was killed.

He was educated at Radley College near Abingdon, Oxfordshire as an Exhibitioner from 1909-13. Known as Billy (his middle name being William), he played cricket for the school XI and is remembered by his school "for his store of information on all matters connected with cricket." Radley match reports show him to have "some pace and accuracy and a bit of swing – if his tearaway action will permit of increased accuracy. A hard-working cricketer, useful in the field and not to be despised as eleventh batsman." A poignant photograph of the Radley XI from 1913 contains Lane-Joynt and a staggering five other team mates who all perished in the Great War.

On leaving Radley he produced the 142-page book *The Public School Cricket Yearbook* which was extremely well received. His enthusiasm for his subject gripped many critics, and in the book he announced plans to deal fully in the 1915 edition with the leading preparatory schools,

Old Boy cricket and the various systems of coaching. Sadly, of course there was to be no 1915 edition. He had earlier contributed 14 pages of international cricket statistics to *Ayres' Cricket Companion* for 1912, largely concerning matches between England and Australia. For the 1913 edition he provided nine pages on Northamptonshire Cricket. Northants, who had finished second in the Championship the year before, was an unfashionable county about which little had been written. Lane-Joynt comments in his piece that "the records of this most interesting county are very incomplete, and no consecutive narrative of the county's cricket is possible." Clearly Albert was something of a cricket "badger" in modern parlance.

A member of Surrey in 1912 and 1914, but not in 1913, he played for the Surrey Club and Ground XI and Gentlemen of Surrey in 1914 as well as writing for the periodical *Cricket* in 1913 for which he contributed *"Public School Prospects"* in the spring and *"Public School Cricket"* in the autumn, the latter being considered first-rate. He worked from his home, Dodsley Gate in Midhurst, Sussex and anticipated going up to Oxford University in October 1914. Instead he enlisted almost as soon as war broke out and was commissioned in the 3rd battalion of the

Dorsetshire Regiment, subsequently joining up with the Machine Gun Corps where he became proficient. He was killed instantly by a bullet from a German sniper at Givenchy in the Ypres Salient in his twenty-first year carrying out, according to his colonel "a dangerous job for which he had volunteered."

An article on him in the *Cricketer* in February 1977 opines that Lane-Joynt was "the most promising cricketer-writer to die [in the Great War]," and says of *The Public School Cricket Yearbook:* "the editor's mature critiques of the schools and enthusiasm for his project – the first of its kind – is gripping." It goes on to make reference to his name being on the war memorial at The Oval.

He is also featured in a touching tribute available on Youtube called "Knock 'em for six: a cricketer goes to war" which features photographs of Lane-Joynt looking far more mature and serious than any boy of 19 or 20 should.

His obituary in the 1917 *Wisden Almanack* somewhat succinctly reads: "Killed on February 26. He played in the Radley XI in 1913, scoring 66 runs with an average of 13.20 and taking 12 wickets for 19.17 runs each, and also for Surrey Club and ground. In 1914 he edited a publication on Public School Cricket during 1913."

•••••••••••••••••••••••••••••••••••••

Of all the photographs that I have obtained of casualties listed on the war memorial, this is the clearest, the best composed and my favourite. If you look carefully you will see that Lane-Joynt is wearing *pince nez* spectacles, popular in the 19th century, which have no arms to secure them over the ears. He is wearing an example of the hard bridge style, which has a solid bridge piece over the nose.

Guards Cemetery, Cuinchy, Pas de Calais, France.

Lane-Joynt is buried in the same cemetery as Dudley Jewell and died just over a month after him. At the base of his cream Commonwealth War Graves Commission headstone are the words: "Heaven is by the young invaded. Their laughter in the house of God." It also shows that he was attached to the Machine Gun Corps.

Richard Percy Lewis

Lieutenant Colonel, Devonshire Regiment.

Died September 7th 1915, age 43.

Buried in Ypres Reservoir Cemetery, Ypres, West Vlaanderen, Belgium.

Lewis was born on March 10th 1874 in Kensington, London, the son of Richard, a barrister-in-law and grandson of JA Kinglake, a serjeant-at-law (an order of barristers at the English bar). He was educated at Winchester and University College, Oxford, although he was never awarded an Honours degree while he was there. He was a member of Surrey from 1893-1914, being shown as an overseas member from 1901-08 and 1911-12. He was also a member of MCC in 1893 and whilst at Oxford was an active member of The Shakespeare Club, an exclusive dining club.

He played cricket for Winchester School from 1891-92, kept wicket for Oxford University between 1894 and 1896 and played 36 first-class matches in a 13-year career as a right-hand batsman during which he scored 134 runs in 58 innings at 3.62 with a top score of 27*, held 55 catches and made 27 stumpings. Those indeed were the days of specialist, non-batting wicket-keepers.

He toured the West Indies in 1897 with Priestley and also played a lot of military cricket. Records show that he played first-class cricket for Oxford University from 1894-95, MCC from 1898-1907 and Middlesex in 1898. His initial first-class match was for Oxford University against AJ Webbe's XI at The Parks in May 1894 and his last was for MCC against Leicestershire at Lord's in May 1907. Between these matches he played for Middlesex in 1898, Gentlemen, AJ Priestley's XI, AJ Webbe's XI and Oxford University Past and Present. He also played lesser matches for Surrey and Surrey second XI, Wimbledon and Winchester College. His two matches for Surrey came in the 1892 season; against Derbyshire at The Oval and Essex at Leyton, but neither was deemed to be first-class.

When the South African war broke out he enrolled with the City Imperial Volunteers and saw action in the Orange Free State. In 1904 he was appointed to the Central Africa Battalion of the King's African Rifles and was part of the Nandi Expedition of 1905-06 receiving a mention in despatches. In 1908 he joined the Egyptian Army and stayed in the country as an intelligence officer in Egypt. He obtained a commission in 1910.

Lewis's obituary in the 1918 *Wisden Almanack* reads: "born March 10, 1874 (according to Winchester and Oxford Register), died of wounds, September 9. Had previously been wounded. Winchester XI, 1891, 1892; Surrey XI, 1892;

Middlesex XI, 1898; Oxford University, 1894-95-96. West Indies with Priestley's team to West Indies, 1897. Played much Military cricket, for Devon Regt., King's African Rifles, Egyptian Army, etc. Lewis seemed likely at one time to be a great wicket-keeper. At Winchester he was spoken of as a coming MacGregor, but it cannot be said that he quite fulfilled his early promise. His ability was beyond question, but his hands would not stand the hard work of first-class matches, and when they went wrong he had bad days. He had no pretensions as a batsman, and in the University match in 1894 he was very pleased that he managed to stay for a couple of overs, enabling Charles Fry to add seventeen runs and complete his hundred. Served in the South African War. Member of MCC since 1893."

There is mention of his death in *The Times* under a sub-title "Died of Wounds" which ends: "Beloved nephew of the late Rev. FC Kinglake, Rector of Monkton Taunton and of Mrs Kinglake of Batheaston Lodge, Bath. Deeply mourned."

Of the 48 casualties listed on the war memorial, he is the only Lieutenant Colonel and the highest ranking casualty.

••••••••••••••••••••••••••••••••••••••

Lewis is the only casualty on the war memorial in *Famous Cricketers and Cricket Grounds* published in 1895 by Charles Alcock (1842-1907) which contains many large photographs of cricketers of the era. Alcock was the Secretary of Surrey CCC from 1872-1907 and the subject of a biography by Keith Booth, the former Surrey CCC scorer.

Ypres Reservoir Cemetery, Ypres, Belgium.

This cemetery, begun in October 1915 and used until after the Armistice, is just outside Ypres to the northwest and the result of three cemeteries combined. There are 2,613 Commonwealth casualties from the Great War commemorated or buried here, although 1,034 of those buried are unidentified. Ypres was destroyed more completely than any other similar sized town near the Western Front, but is now home to an excellent war museum.

Edward Longton

Second Lieutenant, Essex Regiment.

Died June 6th 1915, age 19.

Listed on the Helles Memorial, Gallipoli Peninsula, Turkey.

Longton was born on April 24th 1896, in the Steyning area of Sussex, the eldest son of George and Ella. The latter was the daughter of Major Pontifex of Guildford, Surrey.

He was educated at Westminster School, London, from April 29th 1909 to July 1914 and features heavily in cricket match reports in *The Elizabethan,* the school magazine.

On the 1911 census he is a schoolboy aged 14 and living with his cousin, Richard Leach and his family at Norton House, Wragg Castle Lane, Pitchcomb, Stroud, Gloucestershire.

He did not play any first-class cricket, but did turn out for Westminster School in 1914. In their fixture against Radley College he batted at No.9 and scored 19* and against Charterhouse School he batted at No.6 and scored nine, although in neither match did he bowl. He was a schoolboy member of Surrey from 1911-14, but, like Sills, never reached an age old enough that allowed him to be a full member.

His name was featured in the *London Gazette* on December 29th 1914, which notified that the following day he would be promoted to Second Lieutenant on probation, aged only 18 and a half. He featured in the same publication on June 8th 1915 when he was confirmed in that rank. His medal index card shows that he served in the Balkans and that in 1922 his mother's address was 10 Bigwood Avenue, Hove, Sussex.

The CWGC has very few details about him and worse, the location of his grave is unknown, so he is listed on the famous Helles memorial to those with no known grave. He went to Gallipoli in May 1915 and was killed in the Dardanelles the following month. Clearly his death took a long time to filter through.

His obituary in the 1916 *Wisden Almanack* records: "was reported killed in October in the Dardanelles having previously been stated to be missing. He was in the Westminster School XI in 1914, making 178 runs with an average of 25.42. Against Charterhouse he scored only 9."

Longton is one of the youngest casualties listed on the war memorial. He left school in 1914 and was dead less than a year later.

•••

Helles Memorial, Gallipoli, Turkey.

Longton is listed on this war memorial in Gallipoli, which serves as a memorial for those killed in the Commonwealth battle for the Gallipoli campaign and for those who have no known grave. The memorial bears more than 21,000 names.

Alan Marshal

Private, Australian Infantry (A.I.F.).

Died July 23rd 1915, age 32.

Buried in Pieta Military Cemetery, Malta.

Marshal was born on June 12th 1883 in Warwick, Queensland, Australia. His parents Samuel and Agnes, moved to Brisbane when he was four years old and he was educated at South Brisbane State School and Brisbane Grammar School. His father had been born in Lincolnshire and then emigrated to Australia. A precocious talent, he began playing grade cricket at just 14 years old.

Along with Cattley he is one of just two Privates to be listed on the memorial and both of their ranks have been omitted. He is also one of just three on it to have his first name shown; the others being John Howell and Guy Wormald.

Marshal is the only Australian on the memorial and of those with an obituary in *Wisden Alamanack* his, along with that of John Raphael, is the longest. He would possibly be one of a small number on the memorial known to current Surrey CCC members and was arguably the most talented cricketer of the forty-eight men featured in this book, attaining the distinction of being a *Wisden Alamanack* Cricketer of the Year in 1909.

He initially played for South Brisbane CC but during the 1902-03 season joined the Paddington club in Sydney to further his cricketing education. He returned to Brisbane in 1903-04 and was chosen to play for Queensland, for whom he played a total of 11 matches, before sailing to England in 1905 to gain further experience. He then played for London County and later for Surrey (98 matches from 1907-10). In 1905 he scored 2,752 runs for London County at 56.16 and took 118 wickets at 16.41. The following season he scored 3,578 runs at 76.12 and took 167 wickets at 14.10 for the same team. In 1906 he scored 300* against Croydon, 219 against Norbury and 204* against Cyphers.

He was six feet, three inches tall, a hard-hitting batsman and a fast-medium bowler who qualified by residence to play for Surrey, making his first appearance for the county in May 1907 against WG Grace's XI at The Oval. He scored three runs in his one visit to the crease, but did not bowl as Surrey won a low-scoring match by 9 wickets. The following season, during which he was capped, he amassed 1,931 runs at over 40. He scored heavily in 1909, but at a lower average and was suspended for some matches by the committee after an incident at Chesterfield during the match against Derbyshire, although the committee did not give their reasons for taking this action. However, mention is made in

Jack Hobbs' autobiography, published in 1935, that Marshal and some teammates had been heading and kicking a football about in the street en route to their hotel. A police officer asked for his name and Marshal refused to give it so was taken to the police station. The matter was not pursued any further. After a few matches in 1910 his contract was terminated and he returned to Australia where he again played for Queensland.

Marshal's first-class career record was: 119 matches, 198 innings, 13 not-outs, 5,177 runs, highest score 176, average 27.98. He held 114 catches and took 119 wickets for 2,718 runs at 22.84. His best return was 7-41.

His obituary in *Wisden Alamanack* is too long to reproduce in full, but it refers to him as "a cricketer of unfulfilled promise" and adds that "a hitter of greater natural powers has seldom been seen." The good book continues: "In 1907 he made over a thousand runs for Surrey, but there was a certain restraint in his play. For the moment he was feeling his way. In 1908 he showed all that he could do. He had a splendid season for Surrey, scoring 1,884 with an average of 40 in all matches for the county and finishing second only to Hayward. Five times he exceeded the hundred, an innings of 108 against Middlesex at The Oval being a marvel of powerful driving. When the season ended his place among the great players of the day seemed assured... The future looked bright indeed for him, but he never again reached the same level. At the height of the season of 1909 the Surrey committee suspended him for a time and in the following year they terminated his engagement. Marshal returned to Queensland and played cricket, but without doing anything exceptional. He sailed for Australia on September 12th 1910, and on the day before his departure played a magnificent innings of 259* for Whitcomb Wanderers v W. Jones XI, at Acton, hitting thirteen 6s and thirty-six 4s. Earlier in the season – at Ashford (Middlesex) on July

7 – he had taken all ten wickets in an innings for 28 runs for AH Marriott's XI v Ashford."

He was one of the many Australian troops sent to Gallipoli where he caught enteric fever. He was taken to Malta, treated in Imtarfa Military Hospital, but died there and is buried a mile southwest of the capital Valletta. His death was reported in *The Times* on August 4th 1915.

CWGC records comment: "The earth is shallow on Malta and during both wars, many joint or collective burials were made as graves had to be cut into the underlying rock. From the spring of 1915, the hospitals and convalescent depots established on the islands of Malta and Gozo dealt with over 135,000 sick and wounded, chiefly from the campaigns in Gallipoli and Salonika. There are 1,303 Commonwealth casualties of the First World War buried or commemorated at Pieta Military Cemetery."

He was the great-uncle of actor Alan Marshal (1909-1961), who co-starred alongside Mae West, Greta Garbo and Marlene Dietrich in a glittering film career.

●●

Marshal is one of the most well-known of those listed on the war memorial, thus photographs of him are much easier to come by. I am particularly fond of this one of him in a Surrey CCC cap and blazer.

Surrey County Cricket Club, Kennington, London.

STRUDWICK H	1903	1902-1927	E
WALKER L	1903	1900-1903	G
BAKER A	1904	1900-1907	P
CHINNERY H B	1904	1897-1904	
HARPER L V	1904	1904	S
LORD DALMENY	1904	1903-1908	
McDONELL H C	1904	1901-1904	
RAPHAEL J E	1904	1903-1909	
SHEPPARD R A	1904	1904-1905	
DAVIS W E	1905	1903-1911	
HOBBS J B	1905	1905-1934	
KNOX N A	1905	1904-1910	
BUSH H S	1906	1901-1912	
CRAWFORD J N	1906	1904-1921	
MAY P R	1906	1902-1909	
RUSHBY T	1906	1903-1921	
DUCAT A	1908	1906-1931	
HITCH J W	1908	1907-1925	
KIRK E C	1908	1906-1921	
MARSHAL A	1908	1907-1910	
BIRD M C	1909	1909-1921	
PLATT G J W	1909	1906-1914	
ABEL W J	1910	1909-1926	
CAMPBELL I P F	1910	1910-1927	
GOATLY E G	1911	1901-1914	
HARRISON H S	1911	1909-1923	

This impressive memorial is affixed to the rear of the pavilion after the recent restoration work. It shows players capped by Surrey, when they were capped and between which years they played for the county. This photograph shows the names of Harry Chinnery, Alan Marshal and John Raphael, who all perished in the Great War.

Harold Gostwyck May

Second Lieutenant, Dorsetshire Regiment.

Died March 27th 1915, age 27.

Buried in Boulogne Eastern Cemetery, Pas de Calais, France.

May was born in spring 1887 in Croydon, Surrey, the son of Richard and Emma of "Sherborne", 77 Woodside Green, South Norwood, London. There is a war memorial on the local green, but there are no names listed on it. He was baptised on June 13th 1887 at St Andrews' Church, Croydon, Surrey.

May was educated at Sherborne School in Dorset where he was a member of Mr Bell's house from 1902-07 and in the cricket XI from 1904-07 (captain 1906-07) as well as the rugby XV 1905-07. He was also a school prefect and returned to teach at the school in the Christmas term of 1914.

He did not play any first-class cricket, although he was selected for Young Amateurs against Young Professionals of Surrey at The Oval on August 23rd and 24th 1905, scoring 12 and three batting at No.8 as his team lost by an innings and 80 runs in a thirteen-a-side match. The same season, on September 5th, he played for Young Amateurs of Surrey against Nork Park at Nork Park. Going in at No.6 he scored 10 and 24 as his team lost by 72 runs on first innings scores. Guy Wormald, who features in this book, opened the batting and scored one and seven.

Sherborne School sent me a very clear photograph of him in the 1906 school XI. The keen-eyed reader will notice that at the left of the back row is Thomas Bowley (1857-1939), the Surrey bowler who played 76 first-class matches for the county from 1885-91 and who died in Sherborne.

May's obituary featured in the school magazine, *The Shirburnian* in June 1915 and it states: "Unexpected financial straits kept him from Oxford or Cambridge. Having at once to earn his living, he started schoolmastering at Kelly College, while reading for a Dublin degree, proceeding thence to Llandovery, thence to Clifton." Of his time at Sherborne the obituary continues: "He was always in the right place, quietly determined, unaffectedly cheerful, genuinely unselfish. He had a wonderful gift of mimicry, but was totally devoid of malice. To be with him was to feel the influence of sympathy, dutifulness, honour, of an *anima naturaliter Christiana*. His religion was shy, but deeply felt."

He was wounded on a hill near Ypres in Belgium on March 14th 1915 whilst, in the words of his Company Commander, "very gallantly bringing his platoon up into the front trench. He bore the pain with the greatest pluck and filled us all with admiration by his conduct."

The CWGC records show that "Boulogne Eastern Cemetery lies just beyond the eastern corner of the Citadel. The Commonwealth War Graves plot is located down the western edge of the southern section of the cemetery. Unusually, the headstones are laid flat in this cemetery. This is due to the sandy soil."

His obituary in the 1916 *Wisden Almanack* reads: "Died at Boulogne on March 27 of wounds received on March 14, aged 26. A good batsman and excellent wicket-keeper, he was in the Sherborne XI four years, 1904 to 1907, being captain in his last season. His batting whilst at School showed a continued advance, his averages being 9.57, 17.50, 23.11 and 30.69, the last mentioned being the best of the year for the side."

He is commemorated on a war memorial made up of six marble plaques on the left-hand staircase in the entrance hall to the Reading Room at Trinity College, Dublin, as well as on a plaque in the chapel of Sherborne School, and his name appears on the wall of Sherborne School's war memorial staircase that leads to the chapel.

....

A Letter From The Front

Harold May was transported to Boulogne in France by field ambulance and train from where he wrote a long letter to the Sherborne School headmaster from his hospital. In it he says:

"I am on my back with my right leg suspended one foot above me to a cross beam - an awkward position. This is my sixth day here now. I had better start from before I was hit.

"Friday March 12th, we had orders to make as big a splash as possible in the way of activity – firing all night – machine guns here and there – flares going up all over the place, evidently to keep the Germans from reinforcing elsewhere. We heard no more of this flutter, but the Germans seemed to answer us at night quite cheerily, and shelled our trenches a little.

"Next day passed peacefully, but our Brigade had orders to carry out the same fantastic waste of ammunition at 4 a.m..

"On Sunday we were shelled quite a lot during the day; our Company was on an isolated hill with the trench near the brow in front. It isn't safe to keep the men in there by day, so the majority retire into dugouts on the reverse side of the hill till it begins to get dusk. At 5 p.m. on

Sunday I was looking for my dugout, and I noted how the Germans seemed to be shelling all along a line about five hundred yards to the rear of our brigade trenches. This is a well-known trick prior to attack, for it prevents supports coming up. Suddenly a frenzied burst of rifle fire broke out from the trenches. It was only an hour from dusk, so our Captain said to me 'Get the Company into Number [redacted] trench at once.' I got my revolver and clambered along the side of the hill yelling at each cave to turn out. In about two minutes all were outside preparatory to moving up into the trench.

"Suddenly the most awful hail of shrapnel came over the crest at the dugouts. A whole battery fired high velocity shrapnel for over an hour; down came the trees, up came tons of earth. The men scurried up into the trench pretty quick and one shell burst alongside me and sent me toppling down the hill into a pond at the bottom. It felt just like being popped on the thigh at the footer, though of course the shell made a beastly mess of the leg.

"Two men bound me up and I lay there till 6.30 p.m., wondering if the next shell was going to finish me. After dark the stretcher bearers arrived and carried me down to the battalion *dressing station – a precarious task for them, for shelling and general artillery was still 'on'. Two more miles of stretcher and then motor ambulance through Ypres to Poperinghe, where I spent the night.*

"Next day they sent me down here in a hospital train, and here I seem destined to remain. How good it is to see the spring weather starting! I am longing to get back for a short sniff of Sherborne summer air. I don't know if they will invalid me home for a week or two later or keep me on here. I think it right to have 'raised an arm' in this vile war, but I am longing for the peaceful life again and to be able to look on the roofs and high garden walls of Sherborne, the peers of which are not elsewhere to be seen."

Although it is an optimistic and detailed letter, he was to die within a fortnight, so he never saw his country again. He is buried in a cemetery in a town that overlooks The English Channel - so close to home.

••••••••••••••••••••••••••••••••••••••

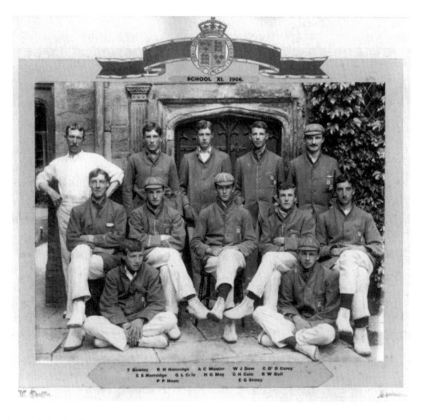

Sherborne School still possess this well composed and very clear photograph of their 1906 cricket team. May is one of only four wearing a cap and is seated in the centre. Thomas Bowley, a bowler for Surrey CCC from 1885-91, is in the white shirt on the left. After a career in which he took 264 first-class wickets he began as cricket coach at Sherborne in 1894, held the post for 17 years and died in Sherborne aged 82. The school are to be commended for keeping this photograph which shows the name of each pupil.

Boulogne Eastern Cemetery, Pas de Calais, France.

May's headstone is unlike most others in that it lies flat, due to the sandy soil in the area. He is buried in this large civil cemetery which is split into two parts and contains 5,577 Commonwealth war graves from the Great War. Boulogne was a main hospital area and until June 1918 the dead from the hospitals there were buried in the cemetery, with the Commonwealth graves forming a narrow strip along one edge.

This is another clear and beautifully composed photograph of May from the Sherborne School archive, taken in May's last year at the school.

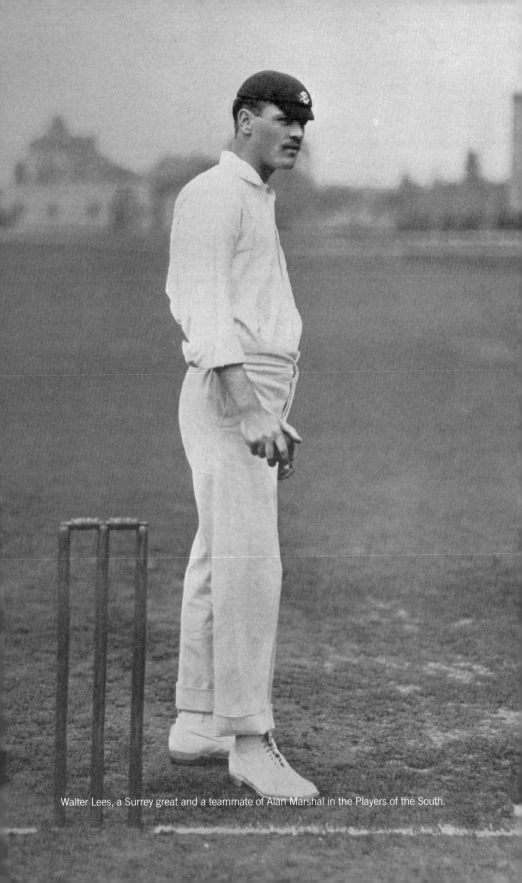
Walter Lees, a Surrey great and a teammate of Alan Marshal in the Players of the South.

Edwin Bertram Myers

Corporal, London Regiment (First Surrey Rifles).

Died September 15th 1916, age 27.

Buried in Adanac Military Cemetery, Miraumont, Somme, France.

Myers was born on July 5th 1889 at Blackheath in Kent, although the CWGC has no details of his next-of-kin or his address, just his service number which was 2259. The 1901 census however, shows that he lived at 12 St Georges Road, Greenwich with his father Edwin Alfred Myers, aged 36, who was a clerk for an electrical engineer and his mother Bertha, also aged 36, born in Pimlico. There are seven further children listed – Edwin B Myers, 12; Norah 11; Philip 9,; Dorothy 7; Ray/Roy 4; Vera 3; and Clifford eight months. Jessie Coxen, aged 20 and a servant from Surfleet, Lincolnshire, lived with the family.

Myers' father got married in autumn 1887 at Woolwich, London, but in early 1907 he was married for a second time to Amy. By this time the family was living at 25 Eversley Road, Charlton.

He played for Surrey Club and Ground in 1907 and 1908, 41 matches for the second XI from 1909-1914 and for the Young Professionals against the Young Amateurs in August 1907 for whom he scored one and 20. Myers played 11 matches for the first team between 1910 and 1914 for whom he scored 217 runs at 13.56, took three wickets for 211 and held three catches. A right-hand batsmen and slow left-arm bowler, he was awarded his cap in 1912. He also played cricket for Charlton in 1907.

The 1911 census shows that on the night of the census he was a visitor at 27 Miskin Road, Dartford, Kent, where his name is given as "Bertram Edwin Myers". The census describes Edwin, then 22, as "a professional cricketer and footballer for Surrey Cricket Club and Crystal Palace Football Club." However Edwin did not play for the Crystal Palace first team. The E. Myers who did was Ernest Myers.

Edwin joined Northfleet Football Club in Kent in 1908 and soon played in front of 4,000 fans against Croydon Common in the fourth qualifying round of the FA Cup. *The South Eastern Gazette* described him as "a colt, a very speedy footballer with a thorough command of the ball. His shots from a position far away near the touchline are notable for their force and accuracy of aim." Northfleet reached the final of the Kent Senior Cup in 1909 although they lost to Maidstone 2-4 in front of a crowd of over 7,000. The following season, 1909/10, they again reached the final of the same competition and beat Chatham 2-0 in front of a crowd of about 6,500. *The South Eastern Gazette* reported Myers as "…one of the stars of the side. Sometimes brilliant. At other times does not show the sparkle that he is known to possess. Often sends in a swinging shot from the touch line with just sufficient screw to curl in and deceive."

Myers moved to Crystal Palace FC in 1910, but returned to Northfleet in 1912 and was again in a successful team that won the Kent Senior Cup against Gravesend in 1913. The match was played at Maidstone in front of a crowd estimated to be 10,000. Due to injury he missed the 1914 Kent Senior Cup final, which Northfleet again lost to Maidstone.

Myers joined the Army and trained at St Albans in Hertfordshire, serving on the Western Front from 1915. On September 10th 1916 he was moved to the front line near High Wood, close to Miraumont. On the day of his death he was part of the support wave of British and Canadian troops in the Battle of Flers-Courcelette. His battalion was all but wiped out; of the 567 soldiers who attacked High Wood, only two officers and 60 men survived.

His obituary in the 1916 *Wisden Almanack* (on the same page as John Nason's who is the next man featured in this book) reads: "Born at Blackheath on July 5, 1889, was killed on September 15. He was a useful all-round cricketer and had been a member of the Oval staff since 1908. He played for the Surrey second XI from 1909 until 1914, and in 1913, when his batting average was 30.33 he played an innings of 142 v Yorkshire 2nd XI at the Oval. He was tried occasionally for the County between 1910 and 1914. His highest score in Club and Ground matches was 196 v Honor Oak in 1911."

His name is on the Stockwell War Memorial in southeast London and on the one in front of St Mark's Church, Kennington, which is opposite the entrance to Oval underground station, about two hundred yards from The Oval cricket ground.

....

St Mark's Church, Kennington, London.

Myers is commemorated on the war memorial in front of this church, which is located opposite Oval underground station and within sight of The Oval cricket ground.

This clear photograph shows the Northfleet Football Club team with the Kent Senior Cup, the Kent League trophy and the Thames and Medway Combination trophy in 1910, after a very successful season. Myers is in the centre of the front row, behind the large shield. The club was formed in 1890 and joined the Kent League in the 1906/07 season which they ended as runners-up before winning the title for the following three seasons. They played at the famous Stonebridge Road ground. They joined the Southern League in 1926/27 and in 1931 became the nursery team for Tottenham Hotspur. In 1946 they merged with Gravesend to form Gravesend and Northfleet FC, who are now known as Ebbsfleet FC and who still play at Stonebridge Road.

Adanac Military Cemetery, Somme, France.

Myers' headstone is of the familiar CWGC cream-coloured style and, like many others, has the insignia of his regiment etched into it. The rectangular cemetery has 3,186 casualties buried within its walls of which 1,986 are Commonwealth casualties and 1,072 are Canadian.

John William Washington Nason

Captain, Royal Flying Corps.

Died December 26th 1916, age 27.

Buried in Vlamertinghe Military Cemetery, Ypres, West Vlaanderen, Belgium.

Nason was born on August 4th 1889 in Corse Grange, Gloucestershire, the son of Dr. Charles and Frederica Nason, who later moved to 23 Grosvenor Crescent, St. Leonard's on Sea, Sussex. Early in 1909, in a faintly Oedipal twist of fate, Nason married another Frederica in King's Norton, Birmingham.

He was educated at University School, Hastings and Cambridge University where he obtained a blue for cricket in 1909 and 1910. His initial first-class match was for Sussex v Warwickshire at Hastings in 1906 in which he scored 53* in his second visit to the crease. In 1913 he began playing for Gloucestershire for whom he scored 139 v Nottinghamshire – the highest score of his first-class career. In all he played 57 first-class matches for Cambridge University, Sussex, Gloucestershire and Gentlemen of the South between 1906 and 1914. He also appeared in other matches for Gentlemen of Sussex, NC Tufnell's XI, Wanderers and a team called Etceteras. I have found no indication that he played for any Surrey XI, but he was a member of the club in 1914.

Nason's sporting gifts were not confined to cricket. A scratch golfer, he played at St. Leonard's Golf Club in Hastings, featuring regularly in the monthly medal matches.

The following is taken from an Adelaide newspaper printed in 1917: "[Nason] joined the army at the outbreak of war, and received his captaincy in November, 1914, transferring to the Royal Flying Corps in January of last year. Capt. Nason, who was born on August 4, 1889, first played cricket for the Sussex County XI at the age of 17 years, and received his blue at Cambridge on his third appearance for the University - earlier than it had ever been awarded before, appearing against Oxford in 1909 and 1910. He also played for the University in Association football. Capt. Nason was invited to play for the Gloucester County XI, and did so for two seasons. He was also a fine golfer."

He is well documented in De Ruvigny's which adds: "He was the son of the late Charles St Stephen Richard Nason, MA, MD... educated at Queens' College, Cambridge... served with the Expeditionary Force in France and Flanders and was killed in action in an aerial flight 26 Dec 1916. His Commanding Officer wrote: 'He was an extremely useful pilot, and his loss will be very keenly felt, not only as regards duty, but as to his friends in the squadron.'"

The long and detailed obituary in the 1917 *Wisden Almanack* adds: "As a lad he was regarded as a player of unusual promise, but, although he made some useful scores, both for the University and Sussex, it cannot be said that he did as well as was expected. In his two matches against Oxford – in 1909 and 1910 – he scored only 32 runs with an average of 10.66. His first appearance for Sussex, against Warwickshire at Hastings in 1906, was marked by a curious incident, for he was allowed to replace Dwyer after that player had bowled five overs, and in his second innings carried out his bat for 53. In 1913 he began to assist Gloucestershire, and in that season played an innings of 139 against Nottinghamshire on the Gloucester ground. When playing for University School v Hastings Post Office in 1908, he opened the innings and when he was bowled after batting for half-an-hour the score sheet read:- JWW Nason b Cox 97; L Inskipp not out, 1; bye, 1 total (1 wkt) 99. He obtained all the first 64 runs and hit three 6s and fourteen 4s."

I am hugely indebted to Jeff Gawthorne, a first cousin once removed of Dorris, whom Nason had married in a hastily convened and sparsely attended ceremony at Hastings Marriage Registry Office in August 1915 "after a whirlwind romance", for sending me an extract from his book *The Gawthornes Of Penang*. In it we discover that the only witnesses at Dorris and Nason's wedding were the bride's mother (who was also present at her two subsequent weddings), and her sister. It would appear that the wedding was frowned upon by Nason's family. The extract is full of colourful details. Nason was "just over 5 feet 5 inches tall and had a fresh complexion, blue eyes and light brown hair." His nickname was Jack within the family but outsiders tended to call him Pat because of his Irish connections. He had developed a passion for motor vehicles, in spite of being injured in a nasty crash in 1914, which led to him becoming a motor mechanic and later pilot, flying reconnaissance missions photographing enemy positions.

However, within 16 months of getting married, Nason was dead; shot down by Lieutenant Alfred Ulmer of the Fliegertruppe (German Air Force). He had failed to inform the War Office of his marriage to Dorris and hadn't written a will. However, in a letter to his mother written in October 1916 he had said that "anything or any money I have" was to be divided between his sister, his brother and his mother. In the absence of an official will, this letter was taken to be a "Soldier's Will" so Dorris was left with just Nason's personal effects, a £250 gratuity and a widow's pension of £100 a year; this despite Nason's property being worth an estimated £8,894 and a further £3,282 – 5s – 9d being left to his brother.

There is a large memorial to him in the Jack Davies Room in the pavilion at Fenner's cricket ground, Cambridge and he is listed on the war memorial inside St Margaret's Church, Corse, Gloucestershire.

●●●

This cricket-themed photograph taken by an unknown photographer is of excellent clarity. Nason is also featured in the military works of de Ruvigny and his write-up, which is accompanied by a small photograph of him in a dark jacket and white collar, gives copious details about his schooldays, military career and ability at various sports.

Fenner's Cricket Ground, Cambridge, Cambridgeshire.

This large black and gold coloured plaque lists the war casualties of both the Cambridge University Cricket Club and the Cambridge University Athletics Club. Nason's name is in the fourth row from the top. It is situated in the Jack Davies room in the pavilion, where the scorers sit at this famous university cricket ground.

St Margaret's Church, Corse, Gloucestershire.

Nason is one of a number in this book whose life has been commemorated with a memorial plaque. This one is by the altar in the church in the village where he was born.

Vlamertinghe Military Cemetary, Ypres, Belgium.

OUR BELOVED SON
BORN AT CORSE GRANGE
GLOS. 1889
TILL HE COME

This cemetery is three miles west of Ypres and contains 1,175 Commonwealth casualties of the Great War. It was started by French troops in 1914 and taken over by Commonwealth forces in April 1915, but further expansion was not possible as nearby land was claimed for a military railway. Nason is buried close to Captain Francis Grenfell, the first British army officer to win the Victoria Cross (August 24th 1914) and war poet Harold Parry, who died aged only 20.

Frank Leslie Nightingale

Second Lieutenant, Lincolnshire Regiment.

Died December 19th 1915, age 34.

Buried in Menin Road South Military Cemetary, Ypres, West Vlaanderen, Belgium.

Nightingale was born on January 30th 1881 in Lambeth, London, the son of Leonard and Agnes of 14 Rodenhurst Road, Clapham, London. His father was an artist and art teacher.

He was educated at Dulwich College Preparatory School from 1890-91, Richmond House School, Sandgate, Kent from 1891-96, Dulwich College from May 1896-July 1900 and London University where he obtained his BA in 1910. At Dulwich College his hobbies were listed as: "Many and various, but chiefly, history, literature of the 18th century, fives, carpentry and cricket. He wanted to undertake a student interpretership in the Far East, but the Russo-Japanese war put paid to this idea."

He played cricket for Dulwich College first XI in 1899 and 1900, Incogniti, Wanderers, the Surrey second XI in 1905 and 1906 for whom he was captain in the latter year, Surrey Colts in May 1901, Young Amateurs between 1900 and 1903, Gentlemen of Surrey in August 1901 and 1906, Surrey Club and Ground in 1901, 1902, 1904 and 1906, Surrey Colts in 1901 and 1902, and for Guildford against Surrey Young Amateurs in 1901, 1902, 1904 and 1906. He also appeared for Dulwich College and Public Schools v Gentlemen of Surrey in August 1900,

for Nightingale's XI v Crawford's XI in 1900 and for Wanderers against Surrey Club and Ground in 1905.

Young Amateurs was a separate team from Surrey Young Amateurs and when he played for Young Amateurs, his school appeared in brackets after his name when the match was reported in the annual yearbook.

In September 1906 he was offered the post of assistant teacher at Dulwich College which he accepted and stayed until he joined the Army in September 1914 as a Private in the Rifle Brigade. He trained on the Isle of Sheppey and volunteered to go to the front in December 1914. He endured the winter at Armienteres, Bailleul and Ploegsteert, but spent two months in hospital near Rouen. He then got a commission in November 1915 and after four days in London returned to the front as a Second Lieutenant in the 7th battalion of the Lincolnshire Regiment, at that time near the Menin Road at Ypres, where he was killed during heavy bombardment.

Nightingale is listed twice on the Dulwich College war memorial; once amongst the ex-pupils and once under "Masters", as well as in their Roll of Honour which says: "Lack of opportunity perhaps prevented him from making a name for himself in first-class cricket, but he was well-known in the best club cricket and was a fine all-round player."

His obituary in the 1916 *Wisden Almanack* reads: "Killed on December 19, 1915, aged 34, was in the Dulwich XI in 1899 and 1900. In the latter year he headed the batting averages with 33.44 and also took twenty wickets for 23.75 runs each. He played occasionally for Surrey 2nd XI, and was well-known in club cricket in the County, especially in the Reigate district."

•••••••••••••••••••••••••••••••••••••

F. L. NIGHTINGALE.

This clear photograph came from the Roll of Honour, published by Dulwich College to commemorate their ex-pupils who were killed in action.

Dulwich College War Memorial, Dulwich, London.

Nightingale is perhaps a unique example of one person appearing twice on the same war memorial. He is listed as an ex-pupil war casualty and on another face, along with three others, under a heading of "Masters".

Harold Thomas Noakes

Second Lieutenant, Royal Flying Corps.

Died July 23rd 1917, age 18.

Buried in Lijssenthoek Cemetery, Poperinge, West Vlaanderen, Belgium.

Noakes was born on June 11th 1899 in Lambeth, London, the son of Thomas, a Civil Servant in the Local Government Board and Ada, who lived at Apsley Lodge, Kimberley Road, Clapham, London. He was baptised at St John's Church, Clapham on August 20th 1899.

The youngest of the casualties on the Surrey memorial, Noakes was educated at Merchant Taylor's School from 1909-16 and on July 15th 1916 played for the school against St Paul's School in a one-day match at West Kensington, the ground of the opposition. Batting at No.9 he scored four not out in a total of 162 all out and held two catches in St Paul's innings of 275-9 declared as his side lost by 113 runs.

Although he did not play first-class cricket, or at any level for the county, there is a Harold T Noakes shown as a schoolboy member of the club between 1908 and 1914. If this is our casualty, then he was aged only nine when he gained membership. This may have been allowed before the Great War, but the 1922 club yearbook states: "No person under the age of 14 years shall be eligible as a member of the club." Perhaps the rules were altered when peace returned?

Although he is shown as being a member of the Royal Flying Corps when killed, he obtained his commission from the Artist's Rifles battalion.

He was only six weeks past his eighteenth birthday when he was killed, but is listed on war memorials in two churches in Clapham; St Andrew's in Landor Road and St John's in Clapham Road. Like Edward Longton in this book, he left school one year and was dead the following summer.

Noakes atended the same school as casualty John Raphael – Merchant Taylor's in Northwood, Hillingdon and they are both listed on the school's war memorial. The two are also buried in the same cemetery, close to the cross of sacrifice and just one row and a matter of yards apart. But whereas Raphael was to cram much into his 35 years, Noakes never got the chance.

•••••••••••••••••••••••••••••••••••••••

THE LATE 2ND LIEUT. HAROLD THOMAS
NOAKES.

Noakes is the youngest casualty listed on the war memorial; killed just a few weeks after his 18th birthday.

St Andrew's Church, Clapham, London.

This large and colourful tiled war memorial is in the entrance room at the rear of this large church. It is an imposing building at the junction of Landor Road and Lingham Street which has a large clock tower on its left side and eight circular windows in a rose-style formation adorning its front. It is the oldest church in Lambeth, being built in 1767 and is possibly the oldest building in the area. It was enlarged in 1810 and remodelled in a Romanesque style in 1867. The front elevation is now a two-tone colour with red rendering and grey brick, although the entire façade is in dire need of cleaning.

St John's Church, Clapham, London.

This disused church is near St Andrew's and similarly has a wide facade which has lost its appeal. The grey framed panel with a white surround is one of two that make up the memorial and is at the front of the building near the altar. There is now a dividing wall which hides it from the main area and although there are no pews in the building, the altar remains, as do the balconies around the upper floor level.

St John's Church, Clapham, London.

ALAN DEVERELL
GEORGE ALBERT DODD
URBAN ROBERT COEN GARDNER
PERCY WILLIAM HUBBARD
SIDNEY NEVILLE JENNINGS
ALBERT LIGHT
ARTHUR LIGHT
OWEN LOVETT
HAROLD NOAKES
BERTIE REGINALD PITT
EVERARD VAUGHAN RIDGE
ALFRED ROSKILLY
WILLIAM GEORGE McKINLEY SCOTT
PERCIVAL HENRY TRINDER
REGINALD PARNHAM RIDLEY
GEORGE HERBERT WEAVER

Noakes' name is to be found on the right-hand panel of the two. It is a shame that all twenty-one names are not listed on one panel. The two panels are a few yards apart and the one on which Noakes is listed does not have a heading, just a list of 16 names.

Sir Henry Leveson-Gower – Surrey CCC Captain 1908-1910.

Erasmus Darwin Parker

Captain, Manchester Regiment.

Died March 20th 1915, age 48.

Buried in Nieuwkerke (Neuve-Eglise) Churchyard, Heuvelland, Belgium.

Parker was born in early 1867 in Great Boughton, Cheshire and despite his first and middle names being rare and being a Captain it is surprising that there are very few details about him to be found. Enquiries with local libraries and the local council drew a blank. The CWGC has no more details about his family background than that his parents were Francis and Cecile Parker.

He was baptised in Eccleston, Cheshire on April 25th 1867 and on the 1871 census he is shown as living at 6 Watergate Street, Chester, Cheshire with his mother, Cecile who is shown as head of the family and five servants.

On the 1911 census he is shown as being single, a barrister and a visitor at The Grand Hotel, Brighton, Sussex with his mother, who is shown as a widow.

An entry from *The Manchester Regiment Gazette* dated May 1915 reports that after an Eton education, he served in his battalion for many years where he was in charge of the signallers and was later a Private Secretary. On retirement from the regiment he took a commission in a different one and fought in the Boer War. He was called back by his original regiment (the Manchester Regiment) and went to France on January 13th 1915. Tragically, he was killed not long after most had realised that they would not "be home for Christmas."

Parker's death was noted in the fabulously detailed war diary of Major Swindell which is available in full at the website westernfrontassociation.com. "Major" was not the author's rank but, curiously, his first name. The male members of his family were named, in a short-lived tradition, after ranks in the military until "all the women in the family got together and put a stop to it."

In Swindell's diary entry for 20th March he writes: "Neuve-Eglise. Finished off soup boxes. Got word from orderly room that Captain Parker was killed at 12 noon. He was known as the father of the company. He was also a millionaire. One private was also killed. They were brought down to Neuve-Eglise and buried there. There were also 7 wounded." The editor of the diary remarks that: "Captain Erasmus Darwin Parker was 48 years old and co-author, with Colonel Willoughby Verner, late of the Rifle Brigade, of The Military Life of HRH George, Duke of Cambridge. He is buried in Nieuwkerke (Neuve Eglise) Churchyard along with the private who was killed. 34-year-old Robert Taylor of C

Company had been born in Dukinfield but had returned home from Christchurch, New Zealand to join the battalion."

Parker did not play any first-class cricket, or seemingly at any noteworthy level, but he was a member of the club from 1909-14, where he is shown as Capt. ED Parker. He was a member of the Army & Navy and Garrick clubs in London and was also a military correspondent, a music critic and a talented oarsman.

At 48 he is the oldest casualty on the war memorial and he was awarded the Victory Medal, British Medal and the 1915 Medal. These medals accompanied any that he would have been awarded for service in South Africa. On his medal index card, his brother's address is shown as White Lodge, Shrewsbury.

In the Great War his battalion served in the trenches opposite Messines between November 1914 and March 1915, then moved to Kemmel and in April, after his death, to Ypres.

•••••••••••••••••••••••••••••••••••••

In Memoriam.

CAPTAIN E. D. PARKER,

Manchester Regiment.

To the great grief of his brother Officers, and of all ranks still serving, and of many who knew him intimately in the Regiment years ago, Captain Erasmus Darwin Parkin was killed in action on the 20th March.

Captain Parker served in the First Battalion (63rd) for many years, and was in charge of the Signallers. He was Private Secretary to the late Under Secretary for War (Lord Hardwicke), and after his retirement from the Regiment held a commission in the Militia (Royal Fusiliers), and took part in the South African War. He was a well-known and popular member of the Army and Navy, and Garrick Clubs, and, for a time Military Correspondent of the *Saturday Review* and *Sunday Times*, and a Musical Critic. An old Etonian, who never lost touch with his old College (whose traditions he so well maintained); a fine oar, and powerful sculler, a man with many real friends, both in the Army and outside it; with a variety of interests, kind-hearted, generous to a fault, " straight " as an arrow, and with a love for this old Regiment, which called to him—and thus he returned voluntarily to serve once more under its colours.

In its ranks he has died—a soldier in his heart, and a fine type of English gentleman, a combination worthy indeed of one, as the old boating song has it, of " the best of Schools."

Floreat Etona—" Dear old Razzie."

H. C. E. W.

Manchester,
27th March, 1915.

Details about this casualty have been hard to find, so I was grateful to be sent this obituary from a May 1915 edition of the *Manchester Regiment Gazette* which outlines his domestic interests and Army career.

Nieuwkerke Churchyard, Heuvelland, Belgium.

Parker is buried in a local churchyard as opposed to one of the more familiar war grave cemeteries. The churchyard, which faces the marketplace, is eight miles south of Ypres and was used by field ambulances and fighting units at various times during the war. It contains 92 Commonwealth burials from the Great War and ten from the Second World War.

Howard Roderick Parkes

Captain, Royal Garrison Artillery.

Died May 28th 1920, age 42.

Buried in Molesey Cemetery, Surrey.

Parkes was born in the summer of 1877 at Aston in Warwickshire and was educated at Uppingham School in Rutland. He played cricket for the school between 1894 and 1896 and at Oxford University for whom he played for the Freshmen and Seniors as well as in trial games whilst studying there from 1897-1900. He married Ada, from Hampton-on-Thames and the CWGC website states that only recent research has established that he is buried in Molesey.

His first important match was for Gentlemen of Surrey against Gentlemen of Netherlands at Richmond in August 1894, although he failed to score in either innings. Between 1896 and 1900 he played a few matches for the Surrey second XI and one match for Warwickshire against Leicestershire in August 1898 for whom he scored one run in the first innings, but did not bat in the second innings. In 1900 he played six first-class matches for London County and in September of the same season for East Molesey v Young Amateurs as well as for Richmond v Young Amateurs and other local teams. In 1904 he played for Shanghai against the Straits Settlements in Hong Kong.

He was a member of the club from 1897-1904, 1907 and 1909-14. His brother-in-law,

Tom Taylor (1878-1960) played 130 first-class matches, of which 82 were for Yorkshire. In 1901 Taylor was a *Wisden Almanack* Cricketer of the Year.

Parkes' obituary in the 1921 *Wisden Almanack* reads: "…who died at Studland, Dorset, on May 28 from the effects of gas-poisoning, contracted in active service in France whilst with the RGA, was in the Uppingham XI in 1894 and the following years. He was a capital batsman and in his last season played a good not out innings of 130 v Incogniti. At Oxford he played for the Freshmen and Seniors and in Trial games, but did not obtain his Blue. In 1900 he assisted London County. From 1897 to 1900 he represented Oxford in the hurdles against Cambridge."

The 1911 census shows him living at Wymondley, Bury near Stevenage, Hertfordshire and his occupation as "Engineer".

In *The Swanage Times and Directory* dated Saturday June 5th 1920 is news of his death. The newspaper reports: "We record with regret the death on May 28th of Captain H.R. Parkes, a frequent visitor to and well known at Studland. He had been staying with Mrs Link, of 'Fairfield', Studland.

"The body was taken from Studland to Swanage on Tuesday morning and from thence by the 12.45pm train to East Molesey. On the breast plate of the coffin were the words 'Howard (Hardie) Roderick Parkes; born May 31st 1877; died May 28th 1920; who made the gracious sacrifice for his country.' The coffin remained in St Paul's Church, East Molesey throughout the night until the following afternoon, when it was removed for internment to the cemetery at West Molesey. The funeral service was conducted by Archdeacon Clark, of St Paul's, East Molesey, a friend of the family.

"The whole of the funeral arrangements were carried out by Mr Clark; manager for Mr Job Smith, Undertaker of Swanage."

His will shows his address as Fairfield, Studland, Dorsetshire and he left effects of £2,882 – 7s – 8d.

He is one of just four listed on the memorial to be definitely buried in England; Chinnery E, Snell and Thorne are the others, although I strongly suspect that Burrell is too.

. . . .

Molesey Cemetery, Surrey.

Parkes is interred under a large cross-topped headstone that sits in the centre of a sizeable burial plot. At the base of the headstone are the words: "To the sacred memory of Howard Roderick Parkes (Hardie), the dearly beloved husband of Ada Louise Parkes, who passed from this world on May 28th 1920, from illness contracted on active service in France two years previously, aged 42."

John Edward Raphael

Lieutenant, King's Royal Rifle Corps.

Died June 11th 1917, age 35.

Buried in Lijssenthoek Military Cemetery, Poperinge, West Vlaanderen, Belgium.

Raphael was born on April 30th 1882 in Brussels, Belgium and died at Remy in the same country. He was the only son of Harriette, of 5 Wild Hatch, Hendon, London and the late Albert Raphael, a multi-millionaire financier who was part of a banking dynasty that at the time rivalled the Rothschilds. In the 1911 painting of Surrey players and members is an Albert Raphael, almost certainly John's father. By this time Albert is an old, bearded man with a stick in his hand and is number 103 on the key to the painting.

Along with Alan Marshal, John Raphael is perhaps one of only two listed on the memorial whose name is familiar to modern day club members. Educated at Streatham School and Merchant Taylor's School, he played for five seasons in the school XI from 1897-1901, achieving prodigious feats that grew ever more impressive with each passing year. In his final season at the school he notched up a massive 1,397 runs at an average of 69 and contributed 76 wickets into the bargain.

However, outside schoolboy cricket his talents took a little while to flourish. In August 1900 at The Oval he opened the batting for Young Amateurs against Young Professionals of Surrey scoring four in a total of 86-7. Frank Nightingale, who is also listed on the memorial, batted at four in the same match. Although Nightingale's mode of dismissal is shown (ct. Rook, b. Black) his score is not.

In 1901 Raphael made his debut for the Surrey second XI against Northamptonshire at The Oval. He played for the second team again in 1902 and 1903 and once for the first team in 1903 against Oxford University, before forcing his way more regularly into the first team the next season.

He played twice for the Surrey second XI in August 1902, against Northamptonshire and Dorset and scored a mere 8, 9, 10 and 32. He also played one match for Surrey Club and Ground against Sutton in August 1902, scoring 16 and taking 0-25 off 6 overs.

He studied at St. John's College, Oxford and played 19 matches for the University from 1903-05 scoring four of his five first-class centuries for them. He also appeared in 39 matches for Surrey between 1903 and 1909 and a total of 77 first-class matches which included appearances for an England XI (against Yorkshire at Harrogate in August 1913), Gentlemen of England,

Gentlemen of the South, HDG Leveson-Gower's XI, London County, MCC and the South. He was a member of the club from 1905-08 as well as being a player for the county.

In his first-class career Raphael amassed 3,717 runs at an average of 30.97, but despite showing great promise as a bowler at school, he picked up only three wickets at a cost of 137 runs each.

He was also an exceptionally fine rugby player, gaining a blue for the sport as a freshman in 1901, and played against Cambridge on four occasions. He won nine full international caps for England, making his debut in 1902 against Wales at Blackheath in the Home Nations Championships and later playing in the Championships of 1905 and 1906. He could play as a centre, full-back or winger and played in Tests against France and New Zealand. He also captained the British Lions on the 1910 tour to Argentina.

As well as being an excellent rugby player and cricketer he was a talented fencer and swimmer, becoming President of the Oxford University Swimming Club in 1904. He also had a strong interest in politics, standing in 1909 as the, albeit unsuccessful, Liberal candidate for Croydon in Surrey.

He was a barrister and gazetted to Second Lieutenant, 9th battalion, The Duke of Wellington's (West Riding Regiment) in September 1914 from where he was transferred to the 18th (Service) battalion, The King's Royal Rifle Corps. Promoted to Lieutenant in December 1914, he was later appointed ADC to Major-General Sir Sydney Lawford KCB 41st Division in October 1915, but died 18 months later at the Number 10 Casualty Clearing Station from wounds received in the battle of Messines Ridge.

His lengthy obituary in the 1918 *Wisden Almanack* states: "The news that John Raphael was dead caused sorrow to a very wide circle of friends. Though he never gained quite the place as a batsman that his deeds as a school-boy had suggested, he was in the cricket field and still more in the world of Rugby football, a distinct personality. Everything he did created more than ordinary interest, his popularity as a man, apart from his ability, counting for much. Naturally great things were expected of him when he went up to Oxford but as a cricketer he began with a set-back. From some cause, after making 47 not out in the Freshmen's match, in 1902, he showed such poor form that he never had any chance of gaining his blue. As a matter of fact he was not tried in a single first-class match. In 1903 his prospects while Oxford played at home were equally dismal. However he got on well for Surrey against Oxford at the Oval, and was given trial for the University against Sussex at Brighton. Seizing the opportunity he played a fine innings of 65, when no one else could do much against the Sussex bowlers and two days before the match with Cambridge at Lord's Mr Findlay gave him his colours. In Surrey cricket Raphael never became a power, but he often played well for the county and when - as the last of various captains - he took charge of the team in 1904 he proved quite a capable leader. Raphael's weakness as a batsman was that he relied too exclusively upon forward play. His method – at any rate when he had to contend against first-rate bowling – demanded an easy wicket. His bowling seemed to leave him after his school days."

A staff officer who was with Raphael when he was wounded is quoted in Du Ruvigny's as saying: "I have seen many men in many parts of the world under all sorts of conditions, but never in my experience have I been so impressed by such a magnificent display of sheer pluck and unselfishness. During the three days he lived he was bright and cheerful, never talked about himself, but was very concerned about his servant, his groom, his horses, and everything but himself."

There is a large plaque to his memory in St Jude-on-the-Hill Church in Hampstead, London. He is also listed on the war memorial at Lord's where he was an MCC member and the one for ex-pupils at Merchant Taylor's School, Northwood, Hillingdon along with Harold Noakes. The two are buried in the same cemetery.

In an extraordinary and touching coda to his life, it was reported in the *Daily Express* on March 27th 2014 that his mother's ashes were buried alongside him at Lijssenthoek military cemetery in 1930. At the time the rules expressly forbade family burials in military cemeteries, but Harriette won over the Head Groundsman, Walter Sutherland. Visiting Raphael's grave in autumn 1929 she explained to Sutherland that she was in poor health, and her dying wish was to be buried with her son. She it was who had overseen the posthumous publication of his 296-page coaching manual *Modern Rugby Football* and had also founded a scholarship in his name at Oxford University.

Thirteen months after the encounter, Sutherland received a package at the cemetery. It contained Harriette's ashes. As the *Daily Express* recounts it: "Without telling a soul he sought out the fallen soldier's tombstone and beside it dug a small hole. Within a few minutes the ashes were buried and the turf replaced. The secret has remained in the workman's family for more than 80 years. Sutherland's son George, now 92, says: 'My father was moved by her determination. He showed me where he had cut out an area of grass and slipped the urn underneath. What he did was in defiance of the rules so he knew he could not mark her name on the grave but he said a short prayer and always said he had done right.'"

....

I was fortunate enough to be sent four photographs of Raphael; two of him in cricket attire and two in military attire. I have chosen one of each.

[By permission of Messrs Geo. Newnes Ltd.

JOHN E. RAPHAEL

Raphael looks remarkably composed in this studio style photograph of him in a striped blazer and scarf.

St Jude's-on-the-Hill Church, Hampstead, London.

Raphael is commemorated by this plaque on the north wall. The church was built between 1909 and 1935 and by the west door is a memorial to the horses killed in the Great War. *The Companion Guide to Outer London* by Simon Jenkins describes it as "Lutyens' ecclesiastical masterpiece." Lutyens designed many war memorials, the most famous being the Whitehall Cenotaph, the Tower Hill memorial for Merchant Navy casualties and the Thiepval memorial in France.

Lijssenthoek Military Cemetary, Poperinge, Belgium.

Raphael died at Remy and is buried in this, the second largest Commonwealth war cemetery in Belgium which contains 9,877 casualties. Of the 9,901 Commonwealth casualties buried within its walls, only 24 are unidentified; the other graves are mostly French and German. It is located eight miles west of Ypres. During the Great War, Lijssenthoek was just out of range of most German guns, so casualty clearing stations were established in the area.

Merchant Taylor's School War Memorial.

The school suffered massive losses of ex-pupils during the Great War and have a huge wooden war memorial to their memory on the first floor. Raphael is listed amongst the eight columns of names. In another column is that of Harold Noakes, the youngest casualty to feature in this book, who attended the same school, albeit over a decade later than Raphael.

Arthur Beddome Read

Lieutenant, Somerset Light Infantry.

Died September 16th 1914, age 23.

Buried in Vailly British Cemetery, Aisne, France.

Read was born in spring 1891 in Sutton, Surrey, the only son of Robert and Maud of "Avalon", Grange Road, Sutton and grandson of Colonel Richard H Beddome (1830-1911) of the Madras Staff Corps. His grandfather was a talented botanist, herpetologist and malacologist who wrote at least 15 papers on reptilia and batrachian and described over 40 new species of reptiles and amphibians.

Read was educated at Shrewsbury Mill Mead School in Shropshire and Sherborne School in Dorset where he was a Colour-Sergeant in the Officer Training Corps. In his distinctly moderate cricketing career he played for the Young Amateurs of Surrey in 1909 against Wanderers on August 28th. Batting at No.7 he failed to score. He also featured against Mitcham on September 1st, scoring one opening the batting and against East Molesey on September 2nd, when he failed to score batting at No.3. He did not bowl in any of these matches. In addition he was a member of Surrey from 1911-13.

The 1911 census shows him as a law student at the Royal Engineer Barracks, Gillingham, Kent aged 20 and a single man. He played as a forward for Richmond rugby club until the 1913-14 season and also for the Army against Sandhurst and Woolwich at the Queen's Club in London.

The Times briefly mentioned his death. He was killed by shrapnel in the Battle of the Aisne and his rank is shown as Second Lieutenant. He had been gazetted to the Special Reserve in April 1912 and commissioned Second Lieutenant in the Somerset Light Infantry in December 1913, joining the 1st battalion at Colchester in January 1914. He was the second on the memorial to die, just six weeks after the British army had engaged in hostilities.

The CWGC says of the immediate area where he is buried: "Vailly-sur-Aisne village was the point at which the 3rd Division crossed the river on 12 September 1914 in the advance from the Marne. It fell to the Germans in 1915. It was retaken by the French on 18 April 1917, lost again in June 1918 and finally captured by the French on 15 September 1918."

He is listed on the war memorial in Sutton, on the war memorial for ex-pupils of the Shrewsbury Mill Meads School, at King Charles the Martyr Church in Tunbridge Wells and the war memorial at Lord's, as he was an MCC member.

••••••••••••••••••••••••••••••••••••••

This photograph of Read in military uniform and white-topped cap was found on www.roll-of-honour. com which has a section devoted to the war memorial at Lord's for MCC members killed in action.

Sutton War Memorial, Surrey.

Read completes the triumvirate of names listed on this large war memorial that are also listed on the war memorial in the Long Room at the headquarters of Surrey CCC.

Charles The Martyr Church, Tunbridge Wells.

This memorial can be found in the church hall, not the church itself.

Wilfred Francis Reay

Lance Corporal, Royal Fusiliers.

Died September 28th 1915, age 24.

Listed on the Thiepval Memorial, Somme, France.

Reay was born on June 12th 1891 in Wallington, Surrey, the son of JH Reay, a retired Civil Servant and Dorothy, whose address was 67 Elm Park Mansions, West Brompton, London.

Reay was employed as an Authorised Clerk in the Stock Exchange and played for Gentlemen of Surrey on August 18th 1910 against Young Amateurs of Surrey. Although he did not bat, he took 2-53 off 19 overs. He played just one first-class match; for Gentlemen of England against Oxford University on June 30th-July 2nd 1910 at Eastbourne. Batting at No.11 he scored five not out and 0* and took 1-51 from 11 overs in the first innings.

His body is not in a marked grave so he is listed on the huge Thiepval Memorial which commemorates those with no known grave. With regard to this large and impressive memorial the CWGC states: "The Thiepval Memorial, the Memorial to the Missing of the Somme, bears the names of more than 72,000 officers and men of the United Kingdom and South African forces who died in the Somme sector before 20 March 1918 and have no known grave. Over 90% of those commemorated died between July and November 1916. The memorial also serves as an Anglo-French Battle Memorial

in recognition of the joint nature of the 1916 offensive and a small cemetery containing equal numbers of Commonwealth and French graves lies at the foot of the memorial."

Like others in this book, mentions can be found of him at espncricinfo.com, and in his case it reads: "Lance-Corpl. Wilfred Francis Reay (Royal Fusiliers), born at Wallington, in Surrey, on June 12, 1891, was killed on October 8, 1915. He was an excellent fast-medium bowler in club cricket, and for the Beddington and Purley Clubs obtained hundreds of wickets. In September, 1912, he took all ten wickets in an innings for 30 runs for Beddington v. Honor Oak on the latter's ground. In June, 1910, he played at Eastbourne for Gentlemen of England v Oxford University. His elder brother, Mr Gilbert Reay, has appeared occasionally for Surrey." There is a conflict in the date of death here and this latter one is the one shown on the Cricketarchive website. His brother Gilbert (1887-1967) played 28 matches for Surrey between 1913 and 1923, as well as one for Gentlemen against Players. He was capped by Surrey in 1920.

••••••••••••••••••••••••••••••••••••••

The Thiepval Memorial, Somme, France.

The huge Thiepval memorial is perhaps the most famous war memorial in France. It serves as a memory to those who have no known grave who are often referred to as "The Missing". On its many panels are carved the names of over 72,000 casualties but even now, if a casualty's body is found and can be identified, his name is removed from this memorial.

Francis Watson Robarts

Second Lieutenant, London Regiment (London Scottish).

Died October 13th 1915, age 33.

Buried in Dud Corner Cemetery, Loos, Pas de Calais, France.

Robarts was born on March 5th 1882 in Woodford, Essex, the son of Nathaniel and Margaret Robarts of 23 Oliver Grove, South Norwood, London.

He was educated at the Whitgift School in South Croydon, Surrey for whom he played cricket and became a Chemical Merchant on leaving school. He was later a partner in Bryce, Robarts and Co., 43-45 Great Tower Street, London EC.

Robarts was a member of the club from 1907-14 and although he did not play any first-class matches he did appear for the Surrey second XI in 1905, Gentlemen of Surrey in 1906, Surrey Wanderers, Buckinghamshire and Norwood. He played for Wanderers against Young Amateurs of Surrey on September 2nd 1911 at The Oval and scored 63 as opener in a team total of 176 in reply to the 212 posted by the Young Amateurs of Surrey. In the opposition XI was Arthur Hickman who is also on the Surrey memorial. He was the secretary of Addiscombe CC and Norwood CC in Surrey, secretary to the Church Committee of St. Andrew's Presbyterian Church, Upper Norwood and Superintendant of New Town Sunday School, Upper Norwood.

He enlisted as a Private in September 1914 and fell near Loos in France the following autumn.

On the website Crystalpalacelocal.co.uk is the following about him: "Enlisted September 1914, died 13 October 1915 in his first regular engagement while leading his platoon in an attack on the German lines near the Lens-La Bassee Road. Sp Mem 14 Dud Corner Cemetery, Loos. He is recorded variously as Superintendent of the New Town Sunday school by one source and Sunday school teacher 1906-9, and Superintendent 1911-15 in a book on the history of St Andrew's called 'The Candlestick' which states 'Keen and faithful at all his work and simply beloved by children.'"

His very brief obituary in the 1916 *Wisden Almanack* reads: "Fell in action in France on October 1, aged 32 [sic]. He was well-known as a batsman in metropolitan club cricket, especially for the Norwood C.C. and the Wanderers."

His name is one of many listed on the colourful and ornate war memorial at Whitgift School to commemorate the loss of their ex-pupils and is also on the one inside the Greek Orthodox church, Westow Street, Upper Norwood, London, SE19, which was once St Andrew's Church.

••••••••••••••••••••••••••••••••••••••

2ND LIEUT. F. W. ROBARTS

This photograph of Robarts came from his alma mater, Whitgift School in Croydon, Surrey. It shows him in military uniform. Sadly his career in the Army lasted only 13 months as he was killed whilst leading an attack on enemy lines.

Whitgift School, Croydon, Surrey.

H.A.Massey
F.R.Matthews
A.C.McAdam
H.B.McMinn
L.W.Middleton
E.H.Mitchell M.C.
W.L.Moojen
G.A.McK.Morant M.C.
L.B.F.Morris
J.S.Müller
R.W.Natusch
A.L.W.Neave
{H.B.New
{A.W.New
J.S.Noble
D.R.Nyren
H.D.R.O'Reilly
W.L.Paine
W.H.Parker
T.O.Pascall
H.W.Pegg
A.C.C.Pendrigh
G.N.E.Pentelow
T.F.Perrin
K.G.Perry

A.H.Petrie
T.S.Pitman
E.A.Planterose
E.J.Porter
W.R.Porter
D.Poulter
T.W.Purves
C.S.Radley
J.S.Reeve
J.A.J.Reid
P.B.Reynolds
E.W.Rigby
F.W.Robarts
L.H.F.Robinson
P.W.Roome
A.E.Ryan M.C.
C.B.Sanderson
R.Saword
H.Sawyer
J.H.Sayer
S.H.Scott
W.Selby D.S.O.
E.S.Shaw
J.C.Shipton
C.P.E.Silcott

I was fortunate to meet the archivist at Whitgift when Surrey played at the school's cricket ground in 2011. He took me into the school building to view this very large memorial to ex-pupils killed in action. It is made up of a few colourful plates which also show those who won gallantry medals, or who were mentioned in despatches. In front of the memorial are glass topped display cabinets which feature more details about those listed on the war memorial.

Greek Orthodox Church, Westow Street, Crystal Palace, London.

This church was once St Andrew's Church, but after its closure the current owners have ensured that the building is still used for worship. It is a large church and richly decorated inside. This large war memorial is affixed to the left-hand wall as you enter, but it has dulled and is in dire need of a clean. Across the top it reads: "In proud and grateful memory of all who gave their lives in the service of their country during the Great War 1914-1919 and of... who worshipped in this church". Underneath their names is: "As a further token of undying gratitude the congregation has endowed the St Andrew's memorial bed in the Norwood Cottage Hospital."

Elvin Alfred Scott M.C.

Lieutenant, Royal Garrison Artillery.

Died April 8th 1916, age 28.

Buried in Maroc British Cemetery, Grenay, Pas de Calais, France.

Scott was a native of Grahamstown in South Africa and born around 1888, although the address for his parents, John and Lizzie, is shown as 56 Nightingale Lane, Balham, London.

He did not play any first-class cricket, nor apparently at any level for Surrey, but he was a schoolboy member of the club from 1909-11.

The 1901 census shows him as a 13 year-old residing with his parents John and Lizzie, two brothers, a sister, an aunt, a great-aunt and two servants at 85 Balham Park Road in Battersea, London. His father's occupation is shown as a "Secretary to Railway Contractors". Come the 1911 census he is shown as residing at 56 Nightingale Lane, Battersea, London, with two brothers and a sister along with four servants.

There are three EA Scott's on the CWGC website who died in 1916, but only one is shown as a Lieutenant with the first name of Elvin, so he can be traced with certainty. He was promoted to Temporary Second Lieutenant on December 9th 1914 and details of his promotion are shown in the *London Gazette* dated December 11th 1914.

He is the only one of the 48 listed on the memorial to have been awarded a gallantry medal; in his case it is the Military Cross (MC). To reiterate my moan on the introduction page, the initials MC are so close to his own initials that his gaining of this prestigious medal can be easily missed.

The circumstances of his actions that led to him being awarded the Military Cross are outlined in the supplement to the *London Gazette* dated April 15th 1916, a week after his death, which reported that Scott, who at the time was a Temporary Lieutenant in the Royal Garrison Artillery "displayed great coolness and courage under heavy fire in removing ammunition from an emplacement which had been set on fire, therefore avoiding much damage and loss of life."

Military Cross medal.

This prestigious and hard-earned medal is the third-level award for gallantry. It was created in 1914 for commissioned officers up to the rank of Captain and for warranted officers. In 1931 it was extended to the rank of Major and to members of the Royal Air Force for actions on the ground.

Victor George Fleetwood Shrapnel

Captain, East Surrey Regiment.

Died March 23rd 1918, age 20.

Listed on the Pozieres Memorial, Somme, France.

Shrapnel was born on June 26th 1897 in Wandsworth, London, the eldest son of Arthur, an accountant, and Kate of 27 Wavertree Road, Streatham Hill, London. He was also great-great grandson of Lieutenant General Henry Shrapnel, the inventor of the shell which is named after him.

He was educated at Wilson's Grammar School which was founded in 1615 by Edward Wilson, Vicar of Camberwell as a grammar school for the sons of his parishioners. The school was located in Camberwell, about a mile south of The Oval. He was captain of the school cricket XI for three seasons as well as Head Boy and when aged only 17 he was elected to an Exhibition in Natural Science at Magdalen College, Oxford. According to Magdalen College records "he was a promising student, of whom the entrance examiners spoke very warmly" but the intervention of war meant that he did not matriculate.

Shrapnel did not play any first-class cricket, or apparently at any level for Surrey and neither was he a member of the club. Initially I could find no clues as to why he is on the memorial, but thought that there may be one in his obituary in the 1919 *Wisden Almanack* which reads succinctly: "Killed March 23, aged 20. Captain

for three years of the XI at Wilson's Grammar School, Camberwell".

Wilson's Grammar School did play occasional matches at The Oval until after the Second World War and there is also the chance that he had a job at the ground too.

Shrapnel's school report of 1914 describes him as "an excellent Captain, to whose keenness the success of the team is largely due. A first-rate medium pace bowler, a good bat and a safe field." In one match in 1914 he took 7-17 in 6.2 overs and in total over his last two seasons at school he amassed a barely credible 197 wickets at an average of 6.75. He was Captain of Chess, a member of the Shooting VIII, broke the school record for the mile and the long jump in 1915 and was a Lance Corporal in the School's Officer Training Corps (forerunner of the Combined Cadet Force (CCF)). To cap it all, this multi-talented all-rounder was also in the football team as well as the debating society.

He was commissioned into the 10th battalion of the East Surrey Regiment in the summer of 1915 and was posted to a Young Officer's Company in County Cork. In December he was promoted to Acting Lieutenant and attached to the 8th Battalion, finally disembarking in France on 22nd February 1917, and joining the 'A' convoy in the trenches near Miraumont, by then a relatively quiet sector of the front. Although "Shrap", as his friends called him, had taken a while to reach France, he was not to be short of action over the next 13 months. Stationed around the Ypres Salient area, Shrapnel went out on regular night reconnaissance patrols and was involved in The Third Battle of Ypres when three convoys from his battalion attempted but failed to capture Westhoek Ridge, incurring large casualties.

Shrapnel was promoted to Acting Captain and put in charge of 'A' convoy in October 1917. He was present but survived the horror of The First Battle of Passchendaele, and despite the odds being stacked against him, was one of the few officers to make it back alive from an ill-conceived counter attack for which he as commended for having "rendered noteworthy service".

But his luck was to run out in March 1918. Operation Michael was the last great German offensive of the war. Shrapnel's battalion was ordered to defend the village of Remigny, nine miles south of St. Quentin, the central pivot of the German attack, but faced with overwhelming numbers and prodigious heavy artillery, they were forced into a series of small retreats before Shrapnel and his convoy finally arrived at the village of Audignicourt, about eight miles from St. Quentin. Stationed on the railway embankment at Menessis about a mile away, Shrapnel was killed by machine gun fire during the initial German attack. The report of the battle commented that Shrapnel "had commanded his Company with conspicuous ability and gallantry since the beginning of October 1917, especially at Poelcapelle on 12th August 1917." A fellow officer wrote to Shrapnel's parents: "He was killed playing the game, like the true sportsman he was. He commanded his men extraordinarily

well at all times, and the high standard of his company reflected great credit on him."

The editorial in the July 1918 edition of *The Wilsonian*, in which news of Shrapnel's death was announced, described him as "a boy of brilliant abilities, shown in the classroom, the cricket and football fields, in the debating society, in the chess team and on the Magazine Committee."

His body lies in an unmarked grave, so he is listed on a war memorial situated in the infamous Somme area. He is also listed on the war memorial at Wilson's Grammar School which is now located at Wallington in Surrey, having moved from Camberwell in 1975. He left £317 – 11s – 1d.

••

Shrapnel's alma mater, Wilson's Grammar School, have kept a worthy amount of material and were able to send me three photographs relating to him, for which I am very grateful. This photograph shows him in cricket attire in the centre of the group with the names of his teammates around the outside.

Pozieres War Memorial, Somme, France.

Shrapnel is one of many hundreds of thousands of war casualties who have no known grave. He is listed along with 14,000 others on this impressive war memorial located close to the scene of many years of ferocious fighting. The CWGC website states: "The Pozieres Memorial commemorates over 14,000 casualties of the United Kingdom and 300 of the South African Forces who have no known grave and who died on the Somme from 21 March to 7 August 1918." The memorial is about four miles northeast of the town of Albert and encloses the Pozieres British Cemetery.

Charles Caldwell Sills

Second Lieutenant, South Wales Borderers.

Died September 26th 1914, age 20.

Listed on the La-Ferte-Sous-Jouarre Memorial, Seine-et-Marne, France.

Sills was born on December 24th 1893 in Wandsworth, London, the son of George, a Barrister-at-Law and HBM Magistrate in Zanzibar, and Alice, who at the time of his death, lived at Coed Maes, Oakham, Rutland. He was the grandson of the late George Sills, Recorder of Lincoln and the great-nephew of the late Colonel John Fletcher Caldwell. He was baptised at St Anne's Church, Wandsworth, London on February 4th 1894 and his parents resided at 2 Windmill Road, Wandsworth.

Sills was educated at Oakham School, Rutland and Sandhurst. At Oakham he was in the cricket XI for five years, being captain in 1911 and 1912 and was also in the rugby XV for two years. He won a double blue at Sandhurst for athletics (high jump) and cricket and scored 103 for Sandhurst against Woolwich in 1913. In 1913 and 1914 he played cricket and rugby for the Aldershot command.

Sills did not play any first-class cricket, but did play for the Surrey Young Amateurs against Gentlemen of Surrey on August 27th 1912. Opening the batting he scored three as his team made 273 to win by 176 on first innings scores. On August 18th 1913 he played as opener again for the same team against Young Professionals of Surrey at The Oval, scoring two and five as his side lost by 16 runs. The next day he scored 55

for them against Young Amateurs of Middlesex as they pulled off victory by a massive 325 runs, and the following day scored four against Gentlemen of Surrey at The Oval in a match his team won by 1 wicket. He was a member of the MCC and is listed on the war memorial at Lord's.

He began at Sandhurst Military College in 1912, was gazetted Second Lieutenant in the South Wales Borderers on September 17th 1913 and went to France with the British Expeditionary Force in August 1914. He served at the Retreat from Mons, the Battle of the Marne and the advance to the Aisne, but was killed near Vendresse whilst his battalion was repelling an attack on their trenches.

His body was not identified so, like Charles Hoare in this book, he is listed on the La-Ferte-Sous-Jouarre Memorial with others who have no known grave.

He was the third soldier on the memorial to be killed in the Great War; only Hoare and Read died before him. Having enlisted so young and been killed as part of the initial response to German hostility, he saw little of the war and little of life.

This photograph was found on the website rutlandmembers.org within a section devoted to remembering Rutland men who perished in the Great War.

La-Fuerte-Sous-Jouarre Memorial, Seine-et-Marne, France.

Sills, like Charles Hoare, is listed on this memorial to those with no known grave. It lists a total of nearly 4,000 men who died in the early part of the Great War and is located about 43 miles east of Paris.

Christopher Snell

Second Lieutenant, Duke of Wellington's (West Riding Regiment).

Died July 14th 1916, age 21.

Buried in Wandsworth (Streatham) Cemetery, London.

Snell was born on February 1st 1895 in Wandsworth, London, the son of the Reverend Bernard and Kate Snell. His address whilst a school student is shown as 94 New Park Road, Brixton Hill, southwest London, although CWGC records show that his parents later resided at 31 Mount Nod Road, Streatham, London.

He was educated at the non-conformist Mill Hill School in London from 1906-12 where he became a senior monitor and played cricket for the school between 1910 and 1912. He went on to study at Wadham College, Oxford. He did not have time to sit any exams at Oxford, but whilst there did play cricket, hockey and tennis for the college in 1913, as well as becoming Secretary of cricket.

Snell did not play any first-class cricket and is one of the three on the memorial that I cannot link to Surrey CCC as a member, player, or by way of a job at the club. However his brother HE Snell, who also attended Mill Hill School and Wadham College, played for Young Amateurs against Surrey Young Professionals at The Oval in 1906 and three matches for Surrey Young Amateurs in the same season. An HS Snell played for Gentlemen of Surrey in 1907 and an E Shirley Snell, who played for the Surrey Club and Ground XI in 1906 and for Gentlemen of

Surrey in 1908, is depicted in the 1911 painting of the players and members. He is number 37 on the key to the painting. So there appears to be a healthy family link with the club.

He enlisted immediately at the outbreak of war, initially into the London Territorial Regiment after which he was commissioned into the Duke of Wellington's and saw his first action on 26th August 1915. He died in Guy's Hospital, London on July 14th 1916 nine days after receiving wounds in France where it appears he spent all of his service.

He is one of the four in this book who were definitely buried in England; in his case it is close to home in Wandsworth (Streatham) Cemetery. His obituary in the 1917 *Wisden Almanack* reads: "Died of wounds at Guy's Hospital on July 14, aged 21. He was in the Mill Hill School XI in 1910 and two following years, and during his last two seasons performed thus:

1911 – 194 runs (average 13.85) and 25 wickets (average 12.12).

1912 – 348 runs (average 26.38) and 31 wickets (average 10.09)."

This studious head and shoulders photograph is to be found in the memorial section of the website for Mill Hill School where Snell was educated.

Wandsworth (Streatham) Cemetery, London.

Snell is one of the four on the war memorial to be buried in England and his damaged headstone, which has lost its cross, tells a sad story. His sister Jenifer Margaret Snell, who died on Christmas Day 1899 aged just six, is buried with him.

The iconic Oval Long Room before the outbreak of the Great War.

Thomas Colegrave Stafford

Captain, Yorkshire Regiment.

Died April 4th 1916, age 43.

Listed on the Kirkee 1914-1918 Memorial, Poona, India.

Stafford was born in 1873 in Camberwell, London, a short distance from The Oval and was one of just a few in this book about whom very little had come to light until I was pointed in the direction of entries in two gazettes that outlined his career and demise. The CWGC records contain no details about his family, education or career.

Further research shows that he was baptised on July 8th 1874 at St John the Evangelist Church in East Dulwich, London and that his parents were Francis and Mary of Crystal Villas, Crystal Palace Road, East Dulwich, London.

He played for Dulwich College v MCC in May 1896, (although a reply from the school stated that they had no record of him attending the school), for Sutton against Surrey Amateurs in September 1907, for Surrey Club and Ground in 1908 and 1912, for Gentlemen of Surrey in 1910 and for Wanderers between 1908 and 1913.

He did not play any first-class cricket, but did play for the Surrey second XI in May 1908 against Yorkshire at The Oval and against Wiltshire in July of the same season at Chippenham. In the latter match, which Wiltshire won by 7 wickets, he scored one run batting at No.5. Henry Blacklidge, who also features in this book,

batted at No.7 in the same match and scored 19 in Surrey's total of 144.

On September 10th 1912 he played for Wanderers against Young Amateurs of Surrey at The Oval and opened the batting, scoring 155 in their total of 306-3 in a drawn match. Francis Gillespie and John Nason, who both feature in this book, were down to bat at No.4 and No.11 respectively for Wanderers in this game. On September 3rd 1913 he opened the batting in the corresponding fixture at the same venue and scored 52 in his team's total of 191 as they won by 2 wickets. He played for Wanderers on numerous occasions and for Calcutta against Europeans, for whom he scored 17 and 32, in a two-day match in Calcutta that began on Christmas Day 1913. The cricket that he played was concentrated around the southeast and southwest London areas and as he played for Calcutta and died three years later in India, I presume that he was a career soldier who served there for long periods, or on more than one occasion.

The *London Gazette* dated September 15th 1916 reports: "Notice is hereby given, that all creditors and other persons having any claims or demands against the estate of Thomas

Colegrave Stafford, late of 294 Ashley Gardens, Westminster in the county of London, deceased (who died on the 2nd day of April 1916, and whose will was proved in the Principal Registry of the Probate Division of His Majesty's High Court of Justice, on the 7th day of September 1916, by John Hugh Cowan of 71 Underhill Road, Dulwich in the county of Surrey, the executor therein named) are hereby required to send the particulars, in writing, of their claims……"

His will showed his address as 224 Ashleigh Gardens, Westminster, London and with effects of £12,094 – 18s – 8d. His executor, John Hugh Cowan, was a deputy under-writer at Lloyds.

His obituary in the 1917 *Wisden Almanack* reads simply: "Died at Ahmednagar, India, on April 2, as the result of a riding accident. He had played a few times for Surrey second XI, and belonged to the Wanderers and Sutton CC."

Stafford is depicted in the 1911 painting of the Surrey CCC players and members and is number 42 on the key. He is wearing a light blue suit and waistcoat and standing in a group of four at the very front, just left of centre. All four are wearing ties, suits and straw boaters. A Sydney Stafford stands next to him and is number 43 on the key.

A Surrey fan watches his team.

Arthur Burrell Thorne

Lieutenant, Royal Air Force.

Died May 8th 1918, age 23.

Buried in St Mary's Church, Heacham, Norfolk.

Thorne was born on March 25th 1895 in Wimbledon, Surrey and was the son of FG Thorne, but the CWGC website gives very few details about him. His age and next-of-kin details are not listed. There is a middle-aged FG Thorne, possibly his father, portrayed in the 1911 painting of the Surrey players and members (number 16 on the key).

He was baptised at St Mary's Church, Wimbledon, Surrey on April 25th 1895 and his parents were Frederick and Mabel. Unfortunately it is not possible to read his address or father's occupation due to the vicar's poor handwriting; an all too familiar bane of the researcher's life.

The 1911 census shows him as a student at Haileybury College, Haileybury, Hertfordshire and he played cricket for the school in 1912 and 1913. In seven matches that I have found recorded, he batted either at No.5 or No.9 and in a match against Wellington College in June 1912 he took five wickets, although the full figures are not shown. He did not play any first-class cricket, but did play for Surrey Young Amateurs on August 12th 1913 against Young Professionals of Surrey at The Oval, scoring 29 and 15. He also took 1-24 and 4-56 as his side lost by 161 runs. Again at The Oval he scored

18 and took 0-2 for the same XI against Young Amateurs of Essex on August 20th 1913, which saw his side win by 268 runs.

Known as "Pat" to his friends, Thorne went to Canada in January 1914 to work in the Canadian Bank of Commerce. When war broke out he was at Gilbert Plains, Manitoba and made an unsuccessful attempted to join the Canadian Expeditionary Force in October 1914, so he returned to England and was commissioned in the Royal Field Artillery. He went to France in February 1915, and during the Battle of Loos was in charge of a trench mortar battery taking two trench mortars into the German trenches during the attack. Joining the Royal Flying Corps on May 1st 1916 he flew as an observer until February 14th 1917. He returned to England, obtained his wings and returned to France in May 1917. On June 25th he got into a spin and crashed during a test flight, completely wrecking the aircraft and causing damage to his ankle that required some bone to be removed. He was in hospital and a convalescent home for several months. In February 1918 he passed a medical and was posted as an instructor to Lincolnshire despite the fact he was still unable to walk without crutches. His ability as a pilot was apparently unimpaired and he was passed fit for General Service. Killed as a result of a collision, an application to return to active service in France was found on his body.

He had married Katherine Thursby in late 1917 and details of their marriage appeared in *The Times,* the wedding taking place at Castle Rising in Norfolk.

Cricketarchive.com reports that he was killed "in a flying accident." His short obituary in the 1919 *Wisden Almanack* reads: "Had been wounded. Born 1895; killed May 8, a result of a collision in the air while engaged in instructing a class in flying. Haileybury XI, 1912 and 1913."

His will states that he died at Grantham, Lincolnshire, but his address is shown as Willows, Heacham, Norfolk. He left effects of £551 – 3s – 7d and his widow Katherine Gwenllian Thorne was the executor.

He is one of just four in this book to be definitely buried in England and in his case, like Esme Chinnery and Howard Parkes, he is interred under a fine headstone with the following inscription on the bottom:

To count the life of battle good

And dear the land that gave you birth

But dearer still the brotherhood

That binds the brave of all the earth.

St Mary's Church, Heacham, Norfolk.

Most war casualties are interred under small cream coloured CWGC headstones, so it is a welcome change to find one with a headstone which is so very bold. The front is embossed with the wings of the RAF. and also: "Sacred to the memory of Lieut. Arthur Burrell Thorne, RFA attached RAF killed in a collision in the air May 8th 1918, aged 23 years."

Carleton Wyndham Tufnell

Lieutenant, Grenadier Guards.

Died November 6th 1914, age 22.

Buried in Zillebeke Churchyard, Ypres, West Vlaanderen, Belgium.

Tufnell was born on August 5th 1892 in Sydenham, Kent, the third son of Carleton and Laura, later of Waterdone Manor, Kenley, Surrey.

He was educated at Eton where he was in Mr Williams' class between February 1905 and February 1911 and later Sandhurst. At Eton he was an excellent athlete. He played cricket for the school in 1910 and 1911 and was captain in the latter year. He played twice against both Harrow and Winchester. He was also Keeper of the Field, Keeper of the Oppidon Wall and Mixed Wall, and President of the Eton Society. He won the Victor Ludorum Prize at athletics and the King's Medal at Officer Training Corps. At Sandhurst he was captain of the cricket, football and athletic teams and played cricket for Household Brigade, MCC and I Zingari. This excellent all round sportsman also played football for Army against the Dutch Army in both England and Holland in 1914-15.

The Cricketarchive website shows that he played for Eton, Household Brigade and the Surrey second XI. His first recorded match was on June 24th 1910 for Eton against Westminster. Batting at No.3 in both innings he scored 10 and 16. He played at least five matches for his school in the 1910 season and

two in 1911, but it appears that he had to wait until May 1914 for the first of three appearances for Household Brigade. On his debut, opening the batting he scored 64 against Butterflies at Burton Court, Chelsea, London in a one-innings match. William Payne-Gallwey and Lord Bernard Charles Gordon Lennox played on his side in this match. Both men were also killed in action in 1914. On the Butterflies team, the openers were Geoffrey Jackson (killed on April 9th 1917) and Frank Gull (August 25th 1918), along with No.7 William Ash (September 29th 1916), No.10 Neville Wells-Cole (January 6th 1918) and No.11 George Sandeman (April 26th 1915). In total, eight men who played in this match didn't make it back from the Great War.

He played once for the Surrey second XI; against Devonshire at Horley on August 2nd and 3rd 1911, opening the batting with Edwin Myers, who also features in this book, and scoring three and six in a drawn match.

Tufnell was gazetted Second Lieutenant in the Second Grenadier Guards on September 4th 1912 and left for France in September 1914. Promoted to Lieutenant, he was wounded near Klein Zillebeke during the first battle of Ypres and died shortly after reaching hospital. He was machine gun officer of his battalion and hit whilst taking up a position.

Tufnell is buried at Zillebeke churchyard cemetery and along with his fallen comrades is the subject of a book by Jerry Murland called *Aristocrats Go To War* in which he writes: "In this secluded spot a typical cross-section of the men who sailed for France in the early months of the war and fought the 1914 battles found their last resting place. There is no doubt that they were men of a different character and disposition to those who followed; they were part of the last legions of Edwardian gentlemen: chivalrous, privileged and stubbornly proud of their traditions. Above all, they epitomised the professional British soldier of 1914, earning the devotion of their men and the respect of their opponents in equal measure. The men recorded in the Zillebeke cemetery register took part in all the decisive engagements of October and November 1914: Langemark, Gheluvelt, Hollebeke, Zandvoorde, Messines and the battle for the woods around Zillebeke. They served principally with Douglas Haig's I Corps and Edmund Allenby's Cavalry Corps. Without exception all of the British officers commemorated at Zillebeke attended public schools before being commissioned and of these, eight passed through Sandhurst. Zillebeke is also more of an 'aristocrats' cemetery' than appears at first glance. Eight officers and their families are listed in Burke's Peerage, one is a Russian aristocratic and three have entries in Burke's Landed Gentry. The remainder either have links to the aristocracy through marriage or are sons of wealthy professional families."

Tufnell is mentioned on the website Westernfrontassociation.com which asks: "So what of 2/Grenadiers who were fighting for their survival along the Brown Road? Once through the gap created by the French retreat, the advancing German infantry quickly enfiladed Number 1 Company which accounted for most of the 75 NCOs and men who were killed and wounded. The timely arrival of 7 Brigade and the subsequent counter attack took the pressure off the battalion but at some point during the counter attack Carleton Tufnell was shot through the throat and died of his wounds soon afterwards. Writing on 8 November, Captain Eben Pike, the battalion's Adjutant, mourned his passing: 'Poor young Tufnell is the second machine gun officer we have had killed and was engaged to a girl in England. Poor chap, he was always so excited about the post coming and getting his letters.'"

He is listed on the war memorial at Lord's as he was a member of MCC and the one at Canterbury cricket ground for the Band of Brothers Cricket Club, as he was born in Kent. A connection with the county is one of the requirements for joining this exclusive club. His father, CF Tufnell, who played for Kent, served on Surrey CCC's Finance Committee from 1912-14.

••

My only regret with this clear photograph is that there is no badge on the cap or shirt to give a clue as to which team he was representing when this was taken.

ETON v. WINCHESTER.

Friday and Saturday, June 23rd and 24th, 1911.

WINCHESTER.

First Innings		Second Innings	
M. Woosnam (Capt.), hit wicket, b Steel	7	c Lister Kaye, b Steel	1
L. T. Morehead, c Campbell, b Perssé	24	b Steel	4
H. Critchley-Salmonson, c and b Perssé	24	c Mulholland, b Boswell	7
J. A. Parke, c Wigan, b Perssé	0	c Perssé, b Lister Kaye	0
T. N. Hone, c Steel, b Perssé	15	c and b Lister Kaye	23
O. de L. Hough, not out	50	l-b-w, b Steel	23
D. F. McConnel, b Steel	0	not out	1
E. G. O. Lillingston, st Tufnell, b Steel	0	b Lister Kaye	0
G. K. Law, b Lister Kaye	14	b Boswell	3
H. G. Johnston, b Boswell	25	c Perssé, b Boswell	7
J. A. L. Stewart, c Boswell, b Perssé	0	b Boswell	0
Extras—b 5, l-b's , w 4, n-b	9	b 7, l-b's 1, w 1, n-b's	9
Total	204	Total	80

Fall of Wicket	1	2	3	4	5	6	7	8	9	10
First Innings	15	55	55	56	100	101	103	128	207	204
Second Innings	2	3	19	53	63	63	65	72	80	80

ETON.

First Innings		Second Innings	
W. T. F. Holland, c Johnston, b Salmonson	11	c Law, b Salmonson	3
D. G. Wigan, c Parke, b C.-Salmonson	6	run out	18
G. R. R. Colman, c McConnel, b Stewart	10	c McConnel, b Salmonson	0
Hon. O. J. A. M. Mulholland, c and b Salmonson	1	c Parke, b Salmonson	6
C. W. Tufnell (Capt.), c Lillingston, b Stewart	16	c Law, b Stewart	57
E. F. Campbell, c Parke, b Hough	21	c Salmonson, b Stewart	103
W. G. K. Boswell, not out	23	b Salmonson	12
A. I. Steel, c Parke, b Salmonson	3	c Johnston, b Parke	0
K. Lister Kaye, c Lillingston, b Hough	4	c McConnel, b Stewart	26
G. L. Davies, c Stewart, b Hough	1	not out	2
B. A. Perssé, run out	0	run out	3
Extras—b 2, l-b , w , n-b's	2	b 10, l-b's 1, w 4, n-b's 2	17
Total	100	Total	246

Fall of Wicket	1	2	3	4	5	6	7	8	9	10
First Innings	15	26	28	38	60	74	81	88	98	100
Second Innings	6	6	17	48	152	197	201	237	241	246

Umpires—Perkins and Bannister.

TELEGRAMS CAN BE SENT FROM TELEGRAPH TENT ON THE GROUNDS.

Telegrams received for visitors will be attached to the Tent.

PLAY—FRIDAY AT 11, SATURDAY AT 10.45. LUNCH 1.30. STUMPS
DRAWN AT 7 EACH DAY.

Price One Penny.

Horatio Spencer Walpole

Lieutenant, Coldstream Guards.

Died April 9th 1918, age 36.

Buried in Bac-du-Sud British Cemetery, Bailleulmont, France.

Walpole was born on July 19th 1881 in Teddington, Middlesex and was the son of the late Henry Spencer Vade-Walpole, a barrister-at-law, and his wife Frances.

He was educated at Eton and New College, Oxford University. After leaving university Walpole worked for Dangerfield, Blythe & Co of 26 Craven Street, Charing Cross moving on to become a solicitor and joining the Inns of Court Officer Training Corps on January 3rd 1916.

On completion of his training he was gazetted to Second Lieutenant in the Coldstream Guards on March 25th 1916 and posted to France in August 1916, but was wounded on September 15th when he was shot in the right forearm. He was promoted to Lieutenant the next day, but his wound was so serious he was taken to a general hospital in Rouen, France for treatment after which he returned to England. He went back to France in August 1917 where the following year he was killed near Arras whilst commanding Number 1 Company of the Battalion, which was in the front line at Boiry St Martin. A German artillery shell landed in the trench in which he was standing and killed him outright.

His Commanding Officer wrote of him: "The regiment has lost in him a most excellent officer, who could always be relied on in any time of stress or trouble. We can ill afford to lose such as he was. His country owes him a special debt, as he gave up so much to fight for her. His brother officers will miss him badly; he was so keen and ready for anything. His personality was so strong, it made itself felt wherever he went, and everybody loved him."

He was heir-presumptive to the two baronies of Walpole and married Dorothea at St Stephen's Church, Gloucester Road, London, S.W. on July 3rd 1906. They went on to have two children, Pamela and Robert. CWGC records show his wife's address as "The Firs," Stevenage, Hertfordshire.

He played for Surrey Club and Ground in 1902 under the surname of Vade-Walpole and in three innings as a later order batsman, scored 12, 10 and four. Against Dorking on July 30th he took 0-20 off 9 overs. In one of these matches, against Leatherhead on August 1st 1902, he was in the same XI as Frank Nightingale, who also features in this book. On July 25th 1902 he played for Kenley against Surrey Club and Ground and took 5-49 off 18 overs as the opening bowler. In 1910 he also played for Oxford University Authentics.

A match for the Club and Ground XI was not enough to guarantee a place on the war memorial, so I assume that he was employed by the club in some capacity, or perhaps he was a benefactor.

There is an excellent plaque to his memory in Trinity Church, Stevenage, Hertfordshire and he is also listed on the war memorial in the town. In St Margaret's Church, Chipstead, Surrey there is a stained glass window to his and his brother's memory and relatives of his are buried close to the church door. Finally in St Andrew's Church, Wickmere, near Aldborough, Norfolk there is a cross to his memory. In the first half of the eighteenth century Wickmere was adopted as their family church by the Walpoles of nearby Wolterton Hall; the dynasty founded by Sir Robert Walpole, Britain's first "Prime Minister".

• •

This rather dark photograph was found in the pages of the works by De Ruvigny, along with a creditable amount of details of his early life, family and military life.

St Margaret's Church, Chipstead, Surrey.

Along with Jewell, Walpole is one of only two on the war memorial whose lives I have found commemorated with a church window. Not far from the church is Walpole Avenue. The window features St. George and St. Michael. Along the bottom is a scroll telling that it is: "To the memory of Thomas Vade-Walpole and Horatio Walpole, the only sons of Henry Vade-Walpole of Stagbury, Chipstead and Freethorpe, Norfolk, both killed in action aged 30 and Frances, his wife."

This clean and shiny plaque is located very close to the altar in this modernised church. It tells that Walpole lived at "The Firs, Stevenage" and that he was "killed in action in the trenches near Arras". It gives concise details as to where he is buried. At the bottom the plaque reads: "Younger son of Frances S.Vade Walpole and the late Henry Spencer Vade-Walpole of Stagbury, Banstead and Freethorpe, Norfolk."

Sir Jeremiah Colman – President of Surrey CCC 1916-1922.

Walter Victor Patrick Charles Whittle

Second Lieutenant, Worcestershire Regiment.

Died April 13th 1915, age 22.

Buried in Bois-Grenier Communal Cemetery, Nord, France.

Whittle was born on August 22nd 1892 in Donaghadee, County Down, Ireland. He was educated initially at Durban High School in South Africa and from 1908-11 at Dulwich College, Southeast London. Sadly only limited details about him are held by the CWGC.

He did not play first-class cricket, nor at any level for the county, but whilst at Dulwich College played for Old Alleynians Rugby Football Club for whom he was captain of the "C" XV in 1912-13. The Surrey yearbooks show that he was a schoolboy member of the club between 1911 and 1912.

Whittle joined the Artist's Rifles at the outbreak of war and went to France in October 1914. He was commissioned as a Second Lieutenant in the 1st battalion, Worcestershire Regiment and was present at the battle of Neuve Chapelle being in charge of the machine guns of the battalion, but was killed at Bois-Grenier.

Dulwich College do not have one of their customary A3-size sheets completed for him, but he is listed on their Roll of Honour for ex-pupils who were killed in action which includes a photograph and career details. He is also listed on the war memorial within the school grounds and the school still have two letters dated 1921 from a relative, believed to be his father, about Walter's short life. His photograph used to hang in the mathematical room at Dulwich College.

The CWGC website states: "Bois-Grenier remained in British hands, though close to the front line, from October 1914 to April 1918, and the earliest British burials were made in the Communal Cemetery. There are now 121 Commonwealth burials of the 1914-18 war commemorated in this site."

The National Probate Calendar Index for 1915 shows that Whittle left a very modest estate of £47 – 5s – 4d.

....

W. V. P. C. WHITTLE.

This clear photograph of a studious looking Whittle came from the Roll of Honour produced by Dulwich College to commemorate their many ex-pupils who were killed in action. The school were also able to supply some details of his short military career.

Dulwich College War Memorial, Dulwich, London.

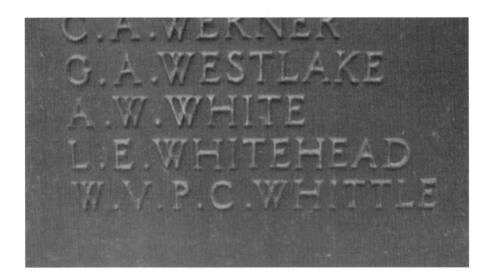

Whittle is the fourth name on this school memorial for ex-pupils who fell during the Great War that can be linked to Surrey CCC. The school were able to supply photographs of all four of these casualties and often a lot of details about their schooldays.

Bois-Grenier Communal Cemetery, Nord, France.

Whittle is one of 121 Commonwealth burials in this village communal cemetery. The village of Bois-Grenier is two miles south of Armentieres and the cemetery is at the southern end of the village.

Guy Wormald

Captain, Lancashire Fusiliers.

Died September 14th 1916, age 32.

Listed on the Doiran Memorial, Doiran, Greece.

Wormald was born on March 5th 1883 near Hanover Square in central London, and baptised on April 14th 1883. He was the son of John and Louisa whose address is shown only as Morden Park, Mitcham, Surrey.

He was educated at Eton and from February 1896 to February 1902 was in Mr Broadbent's class. He played a largely undistinguished part for the school cricket team in June 1902 against Winchester, scoring five and three batting at No.7 and holding two catches as Eton won this two-day match by 4 wickets.

Although he did not play any first-class cricket, he played for Surrey Young Amateurs in 1900, between 1902 and 1905 and again in 1908. He also played for Mitcham in 1904 and 1905 and for HO Dolbey's XI against J Wormald's XI on April 25th 1901 at The Oval when he scored 20 batting at No.5. Esme Chinnery, who features in this book, opened the batting for his side.

In April 1902 he was selected to play for J Wormald's XI against WT Graburn's XI at The Oval. Batting at No.4 he scored three and took 0-13 off 5 overs as the opposition won by 4 wickets. Esme Chinnery was again in his XI and scored 14 batting at No.7 and took 0-11

off two overs. He was also a member of the club from 1903-08.

Three Wormalds have played first-class cricket. John (1882-1957) played for Eton in 1899 and 1900, Gentlemen of Surrey in 1900, Middlesex from 1910-12 and MCC in 1912. Edward (1848-1928) played one match for Kent in 1870 and Alfred played for Yorkshire from 1885-91. Others with this surname played lesser level cricket for Harrow School, Oxford University, Sevenoaks, Royal Military College and Sandhurst amongst others, so perhaps they were relatives.

His marriage to Doris Kindersley, daughter of Edward Kindersley on January 2nd 1912 at Tincleton in Dorset, was reported in the Christmas Day 1911 edition of *The Times*.

On the 1911 census his career is shown as "Barrister" with chambers in New Square, Lincoln's Inn, London. In his 1916 Probate his address was shown as 12 Pembridge Gardens, Kensington and New Square, Lincoln's Inn, although his widow's address on the medal index card is Gorgate Hall in Dereham, Norfolk.

CWGC records show that he was the husband of Doris, of 6 Burwood Place, Hyde Park,

London whom he had married in Dorchester in early 1912.

Wormald left for Salonica on September 4th 1915 and his son, Alan Guy (who was himself to die in combat aged 26 in 1942 fighting in Palestine), was born 12 days later. He was killed at Machukovo leading 'A' Company into battle. His body was not identified and he is listed on the Doiran memorial in the Greek village of that name. CWGC records state: "The Memorial stands near Doiran Military Cemetery in the north of Greece close to the Yugoslav frontier and near the shore of Lake Doiran. It is approximately two kilometres from the village of Doiran and is reached via a farm track after turning left in the village by a large taverna."

His brief obituary in the 1917 *Wisden Almanack* reads: "Killed on September 14, aged 33, was in the Eton XI in 1902, when he made 84 runs with an average of 10.50. He did not play against Harrow, and made 5 and 3 v Winchester."

There is a large cream coloured marble wall-tablet to his memory on a lower floor at the Union Jack Club in Waterloo, London which was dedicated by Mrs E Wormald, but I feel that there is a lot about this man that has not come to light as a good education, a good rank in the army and some attainment on the cricket field all point this way. Enquiries with the historian of the Lancashire Fusiliers elucidated some details about his death, but also the response: "I am sorry I have so little on him."

His estate was valued at £32,073; a colossal amount for this period.

•••••••••••••••••••••••••••••••••••••

MITCHAM v. T. RICHARDSON'S XI.
September, 1904.

Back Row:- H. Eve   G. Curtis   A.C. Butler   W. Hussey   B. Cole   H. Britton   A. Batt   A. Stagg   W. Peters

Middle Row:-   A.F. Clarke   T.P. Harvey   H.G. Currie   J. Boxall   G. Wormald   E. Bale

Seated:-   H. Pillinger   C. Haydon   T. Sturtivant

This team photograph is of the Mitcham side for their match in September 1904 against Tom Richardson's XI. Tom Richardson (1870-1912) was a famous Surrey and England cricketer whose life was subject of a recent biography by former Surrey CCC scorer Keith Booth. He died in France at a young age after a very impressive career. Wormald is in the middle row, second from the right.

The Union Jack Club, Waterloo, London.

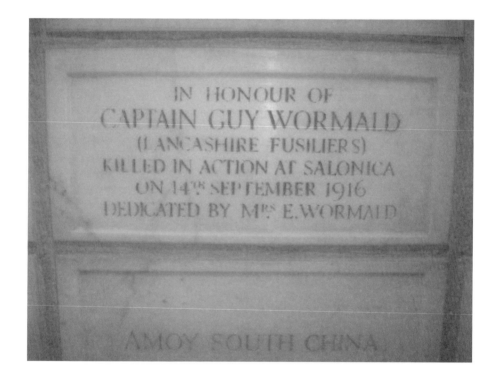

This large stone plaque is on a staircase wall on a lower floor at this famous military club, which is for the use of Non-Commissioned Officers.

Philip Cecil Wynter

Captain, East Surrey Regiment.

Died April 20th 1915, age 35.

Buried in Railway Dugouts Burial Ground, Ypres, West Vlaanderen, Belgium.

Wynter was born on January 31st 1880 in Chelsea, London, the son of Captain Philip HM Wynter (King's Foreign Service Messenger) and Constance Wynter of "The Hays", Ramsden, Oxfordshire. He was baptised at St Saviour's Church, Chelsea, London on March 14th 1880.

In the 1881 census he is aged one and shown living at 41 Ovington Square, Brompton, London, with his parents and four live-in servants. His grandfather, also called Philip, was a Fellow and President of St John's College, Oxford and a Reverend.

In the 1891 census he is 11, a student and living at "The Hays", Hailey, near Witney, Oxfordshire with his parents, two brothers, a sister and two maids. He was educated at Harrow School in Middlesex.

Wynter was due to play for Gentlemen of Surrey against St John's School at Leatherhead on June 17th 1911, but is shown as "absent". St John's School won by 8 wickets. He did however play for the same team against Cane Hill at Coulsdon on July 4th 1914 and opened the batting, scoring 23 as his side lost by 11 runs on first innings scores. During the match he also bowled one over and returned figures of 0-10. In addition, he played for Free Foresters.

He was a Surrey member from 1910-14 and was also an excellent horseman.

He was gazetted Second Lieutenant on December 4th 1901 and joined his battalion at Lucknow the following year. He was promoted to Lieutenant on November 30th 1903 and to Captain on January 26th 1910. He went to France at the end of October 1914 but was invalided home in December, only to return in February 1915. He was killed two months later at Hill 60 which was about three miles southeast of Ypres and made from the soil removed during the construction of the railway line nearby. As it was a small area of raised land in a flat landscape, it had strategic importance in local battles. He was unmarried.

His brother, Captain Francis Wynter, was killed in action in November 1915 at Ctesiphon, 20 miles southeast of Baghdad in Iraq.

••

Philip C. Wynter.

This photograph of Wynter comes from De Ruvigny's five volumes of biographical details of over 26,000 casualties killed in the Great War, compiled by the 9th Marquis de Ruvigny and Raineval. It is often an excellent source of information about a casualty's military career.

Wynter is the last of the three to be found in the 1911 painting of players and members. He is wearing a brown suit and lighter coloured waistcoat. He has a clear complexion and is seated in an upright posture on the far left, towards the front of the members. On the key next to the painting he is number 84.

Railway Dugouts Burial Ground, Ypres, Belgium.

Wynter is one of 2,459 Commonwealth casualties of the Great War buried in this cemetery which is located just over a mile southeast of Ypres. The cemetery is close to where the railway passes on an embankment overlooking a small farm which the troops knew as Transport Farm.

Surrey Yearbook 1917

Annual Report

ANNUAL REPORT.

KENNINGTON OVAL, LONDON, S.E.,
April 17th, 1917.

DEAR SIR,

For the second year in succession no first-class Cricket was played on the Oval. The Ground was, however, in constant use for practice by Members, and was in addition very extensively lent to Military sides for matches and practice, a privilege which was much appreciated. Three Club Games were played, of which 2 were won and 1 lost, the Club sides being drawn from the older Members.

During August a series of matches between the Artists' Rifles and sides selected from the Public Schools proved most interesting, and enabled many of our Members to see some excellent Cricket.

The Committee regret that by the death of Dr. C. C. Blades they have lost one of their most energetic and valued Members, who was first elected to the Committee in 1880, and had served continuously since that date.

The Committee have endeavoured by the exercise of rigid economy to reduce the expenditure to the lowest point, but a saving of £1,000, as will be seen by the annexed accounts, unfortunately only balances the falling off in receipts. They consider, however, that any further economies would be prejudicial to the interests of the Club, and therefore urge Members to continue their support. The thanks of the Club are due to the Artists' Rifles, the Grenadier Guards, and several Members who desire to remain anonymous for donations to the Club.

The following Members of the First and Second Elevens have laid down their lives for their Country :—E. F. Chinnery, H. B. Chinnery, W. J. H. Curwen, F. S. Gillespie, John Howell, A. Marshal, E. B. Myers, F. L. Nightingale, F. W. Robarts, and C. W. Tufnell. J. H. Hunt, a Member of the Committee, has been missing since September, small hopes are entertained of his being alive.

Very few matches were played at The Oval during the war and those that were mainly involved the military and public schools. The yearbooks for 1914-1920 were bound together in one volume, but make interesting reading. Here is part of the annual report in the 1917 yearbook. It mentions those members of the first and second XIs who had been killed in action up to what would have been the start of the 1917 season. Many more were to fall before the war's end.

Surrey Yearbook 1920

Annual Report

It has been decided for the present to play no Club and Ground Matches away from the Oval. Arrangements have been made for a number of inter-Military Matches, during which Military Bands will be in attendance, and the Committee trust that these Fixtures will prove attractive.

The Committee desire to express their sense of the loss that the Club has sustained by the retirement of Mr. W. Findlay, who has been appointed Assistant Secretary to the M.C.C. During the twelve years of his Secretaryship, Mr. Findlay gained the complete confidence of all those with whom he came in contact, has done quite invaluable work, and we congratulate the Committee of the M.C.C. on their choice. The Committee is to be congratulated on having secured Mr. John Shuter as Mr. Findlay's successor. His lengthy services as Cricketer, as Captain, and as a Member of the Committee are so well known as to ensure universal approval of his appointment.

J. J. Reid has been Dressing Room Attendant for twenty-seven years, and in recognition of his long service the Committee has granted him the use of The Oval on July 3rd, 5th, 6th, when a Match will be played for his Benefit between Gentlemen and Players of the South. The hearty co-operation of Members is invited.

The dates for Gentlemen v. Players at the Oval will be June 30th, July 1st and 2nd, and those for the Champion County v. England, September 13th, 14th, 15th and 16th.

The Committee has decided to erect a Memorial in the Pavilion to Members and those otherwise connected with the Club who have fallen during the War. It is essential, to make the Memorial complete, to have every name. The Committee are sending out a list of the names they know and will be grateful to receive any others.

This page covers much of interest: the retirements of Secretary William Findlay and long serving Dressing Room Attendant JJ Reid and the decision to erect a war memorial "to members and those otherwise connected to the club" who fell in the Great War. The committee were keen to get the name of every casualty, so asked members if they knew of any more who could be added to those of whom they were already aware.

Surrey Yearbook 1921

Annual Report

ANNUAL REPORT.

KENNINGTON OVAL, LONDON, S.E. 11.,
April 1st, 1921.

DEAR SIR,

The Cricket Season of 1920 proved highly successful. The First Eleven played very good cricket and gained fourth place in the County Championship. The Committee feels it difficult to particularize where there were so many individual performances of merit, but the batting of Hobbs and Sandham, the wicket-keeping of Strudwick and the fielding of the whole side reached an exceptionally high standard. Four members of the Eleven, Mr. P. G. H. Fender, Hobbs, Strudwick and Hitch accompanied the M.C.C. team to Australia.

The thanks of the Club are due to Mr. C. T. A. Wilkinson and to Mr. P. G. H. Fender for successfully captaining the side.

Of the twenty-four matches played in the First Class Championship, fifteen were won outright, two won on the first innings, six lost and one drawn.

Of the twenty-five matches played by the First Eleven, fifteen were won outright, three won on the first innings, six lost and one drawn.

Of the ten matches played in the Minor Counties' Championship, one was won outright, one won on the first innings, six lost and two drawn.

The thanks of the Club are due to Mr. A. W. F. Rutty for captaining the Second Eleven.

During 1920, 2,860 Members paid subscriptions, as against 2,401 in 1919, and the attendances were the best on record.

Expenditure amounted to £26,074 15s. 7d. against receipts amounting to £29,976 10s. 3d., showing a credit balance of £3,901 14s. 8d. ; so satisfactory a result cannot be expected in normal times.

Acting upon a wish expressed by Members, the Committe has placed in the Pavilion a Memorial Panel recording the names of Members of the Club and Surrey Cricketers who lost their lives in the War. The Memorial will be unveiled by the President at the Annual General Meeting.

The annual report starts with a matter-of-fact appraisal of the previous season and details how many members paid their subscriptions as against the total in 1919. A healthy number paid their subscription throughout the war years, despite there being no county cricket. The ninth paragraph mentions the planned unveiling by the President (Jeremiah Colman) of the "Memorial Panel" at the forthcoming Annual General Meeting.

Surrey fans stroll on the Oval outfield during a break in play.

John Raphael's Travel Journal

From his own personal diary

A TOUR ROUND THE WORLD, 1910–1911.

It was a distinctly raw morning at the end of November, 1910, when my cousin Norman Raphael and I started on our travels. Several Old Merchant Taylors, to whom I should like again to express my gratitude, were at Charing Cross to see us off, and their cheery voices successfully dispelled the gloom that a very unfavourable channel weather report seemed likely to cast over us. Later in the day I was firmly convinced that no vessel had ever before successfully negotiated such a stormy passage as we encountered between Folkestone and Boulogne. I have had reason to alter my opinion since then. We arrived, however, at Marseilles without mishap, and boarded the " Osterley," an Orient Company liner of some 12,000 tons. She was very full; but we had a most comfortable voyage, and needless to say a very excellent time. The first port we touched was Naples, and, as we had the whole day there, we went out to Pompeii, skirting round the foot of Mount Vesuvius. It is a fascinating place. Though a large number of relics have been transferred to the museum of Naples and elsewhere, enough remains to show how sudden must have been the onslaught of the eruption; the preservation of some of the buildings and frescoes is wonderful. An opportunity of visiting Pompeii should on no account be missed. It was not till we had left Port Said that a very decided change in the temperature was noticeable. Fortunately for us, neither in the Red Sea nor in the Indian Ocean was the heat really oppressive. We stuck on a sand bank in the Suez Canal for several hours, and had our first glimpse of proper desert. It is hardly the sort of

*

154   A TOUR ROUND THE WORLD, 1910–1911.

country one would like to live in, but for a short while the vista was by no means unpleasing. The brilliant sun shone through the clearest of clear atmospheres, and while painting them in gorgeous hues, accentuated the bareness of the distant mountains; some scattered palms relieved the dead monotony of the rolling sandy stretches, and an occasional camel showed that life was not altogether extinct. Travellers in tropical climes are sorely tempted to indulge in descriptions of scenic and atmospherical effects, so utterly different in their vivid colouring from anything in England. I shall endeavour to avoid this pitfall, and will content myself by saying that many of the sunsets still haunt my memory. You will always find people who insist that sunrises are the most glorious of all spectacles. Personally, I dislike them intensely; they take place for one thing at such an inconvenient time. It must not of course be thought that I am a late riser. I remember one morning in the Himalayas getting out of bed at three in the morning and riding some ten miles on a most amusing little pony to obtain a view of Mount Everest as the early rays of dawn struck the summit. On account of the altitude it was bitterly cold, and though I pointed out several clouds to some Americans as the object we were searching for, the mist never lifted and we never saw Mount Everest. My cousin, wise man, had resolutely refused to come with me, and I was too depressed when I returned even to tell him falsehoods about the view he had missed. I enjoy that experience in the retrospect, however; it is a pleasure to think that I *have* risen at three o'clock of my own free will. To return to the " Osterley "; we left her at Colombo with many regrets. Ocean life, when you are in the mood for it, is an ideal existence; amusements, it goes without saying, are plentiful and varied; there were some very nice people on board, and weather conditions throughout were all that could be desired. The first person we met in Colombo was H. L. Dowbiggin, who was secretary of the School XV during my first year of captaincy. I had not seen him for twelve years, but he had hardly changed at all. He has done extraordinarily well in the Ceylon Police, and the rapidity of his promotion is shown by the fact that he is now Chief of the force in Colombo. We stopped with him at the Police mess, and he was also very good to us in seeing that we should be well looked after in various parts of the island. Needless to say we were continually coming across and hearing of Old Merchant Taylors during our trip. Practically all of them were doing well, and were a credit to the School and to themselves in their various callings. To show the duties that may fall to the lot of magistrates in these parts a little experience that happened to Willett (Head Monitor 1900–1901) is worth relating. We were staying with him at Galle, an old Dutch settlement in the extreme south, when news came in about lunch-time that he was required in connection with a murder inquiry at some outlying village in his district. The Fates had planned it most awkwardly for him. It was a Thursday, and he had just got leave to be in Colombo on the Saturday to act as best man to Hugh Hunter, an O.M.T. in the South Indian Railway service, who was marrying the sister of Owen, another Old Boy, on the arrival of her boat from England. Though only some forty miles away, how to get there, do his work, and get back in time to catch the only available train to Colombo at 7 a.m. on Saturday was indeed a difficult problem. A police officer and he started about half-past two in the afternoon in an exceedingly rickety vehicle drawn by a pair of what can only be called apologies for horses. In this unpromising conveyance he had to cover nearly thirty miles, mostly uphill, over shocking roads. His only chance of a couple of hours' broken sleep was in a frail canoe that would have to be dragged up against a strong current, and he had then to work his way on foot through five miles of bad going in dense jungle. Despite a lengthy investigation and a chapter of accidents he caught his train with a few minutes to spare. We nearly accompanied him—in another " carriage "—but the sight of the only other available quadrupeds decided us not to do so.

Altogether we were a month in Ceylon, and went over the greater part of it, including the buried cities of the plains. These are being gradually brought to light in the thick scrub of miles and miles of tree jungle, and show what an advanced state of civilisation must have existed there before the Christian era. We had four days' motoring through this extraordinary jungle country, and visited Trincomalee, formerly an important naval base, which has one of the most beautiful harbours in the world. We were in Bombay at the end of January, 1911, and later made for Kathiawar on the North-West coast of India. Here in many ways we had the most interesting time of

156   A TOUR ROUND THE WORLD, 1910–1911.

all, as we were the guests of various native rajahs, and right off the "beaten track." Our host for some delightful weeks was the Jam of Jamnagar, better known to *Taylorian* readers as "Ranji." He does not play much cricket nowadays, but a pretty useful side could have been raised at the time we were with him. In addition to the two Relfs and Killick, who were over to coach the Jamnagar team, "Archie" Maclaren, who was a fellow guest, G. N. Foster and H. L. Simms would also have been available. Now when you stop with native rulers, you do not live in the palace, but in guest-houses. Their religion prevents the greater number of Indian princes from eating at the same table with Englishmen. The Jam Sahib (so he is now called) is of course an exception. Their hospitality therefore is different from what we are accustomed to, but common report does not err in describing it as lavish and generous in the extreme. Exigencies of space forbid my dwelling on the quaint sights that even a casual walk through an Indian city reveals, on our never-to-be-forgotten expedition to the State of Palitana, or on the pleasures and the perils of pig-sticking. I must pass over the architectural glories that give to Delhi, Agra and other places undying fame. Weird, wonderful, and "whiffy" Benares, the dirty but not altogether unpleasing ugliness of the hillmen of the Himalayas, the glorious mountains, and even the mosquitoes that are the bane of the British traveller, can only be mentioned. We left Calcutta not quite a year ago, and had a week in Burma at about the hottest time of the year. A well-known cricketer, when asked about his impressions of a South-African tour he had been engaged on, summed up his experiences with—"Oh my, it was '*ot*." "Them's our sentimengs," as the saying goes, in connection with our journey from Rangoon to Mandalay. We spent, I think, twenty-six days between Calcutta and Hong-Kong. I had weighed myself just before leaving Calcutta, and in light "tussore" clothes was exactly 13 stone; in the same kit I could not touch 12 stone at Hong-Kong. This shows the kind of weather that people in Singapore, for instance, have to contend with. Our objective was Japan, and we reached Kobe in early May. "Charming" is, perhaps, the adjective most suitable in describing Japan. The squalor, the dirt, the decaying buildings and the smells turn the edge of one's pleasure in India and China. In

Japan these drawbacks do not obtrude themselves on the various senses. Everything is bright and cheerful. People laugh continuously, and all seem happy. You find yourself laughing with them, and you cannot help looking on life through rosy spectacles. Kyoto and district pleased us most, but nearly everywhere it was delightful, and in its own way the beauties of the inland sea cannot be surpassed. Several Old Boys are in Japan, and it was a great disappointment only to have met "Nolly" Parham and others just as we were leaving. We celebrated the coronation at Pekin, which, in spite of its horrible dust, its disgusting odours and its general untidiness is just about the most interesting city there is anywhere.

Five weeks later we were in Australia; Tienstin, Chefoo, Wei-hai-wei, Shanghai, Hong-Kong for the second time, Manilla in the Philippines, Thursday Island, a great pearl-fishing centre, and Townsville being among the places we had visited before landing at Brisbane. A taste of "station" life in Queensland, a dash to the Blue Mountains and the wonderful Jenolan Caves in New South Wales and a very jolly visit "up country" in Victoria were some of the variations to our experiences in the large towns of Eastern Australia. In Melbourne we were fully occupied. Very kind friends saw to it that we should have the best of good times, and we had previously known in England some of the aide-de-camps of both Lord Denman, the Commonwealth Governor, and of Sir John Fuller, the Governor of Victoria. What with dinners and at-homes, interviews with the Prime Minister of Australia and other leading politicians, evenings with cricket people, such as Clem Hill, Warwick Armstrong, and quite a number of old 'Varsity Blues, race meetings, golf, football matches, sightseeing, etc., etc., we felt in need of a little rest and quiet by the time we retraced our footsteps to Sydney *en route* for Auckland, New Zealand. The passage to New Zealand was uncomfortable in the extreme. A wretched, top-heavy boat that responded to the slightest motion of a nasty rough sea, a large excess of passengers, including a whole theatrical company, disobliging stewards, and a veritable orgy of sea-sickness on and below decks, are not a happy combination. I gave a further proof, however, of my immunity from "fish-feeding"—an immunity I am glad to say which lasted throughout our travels. We had bad weather the whole time we were in New Zealand and were

158   A TOUR ROUND THE WORLD, 1910–1911.

just too early for the trout fishing, which, from all accounts, must be remarkable sport. We spent some time in the hot spring and geyser district around Rotorua. It is uncanny to see natural boiling water welling up beside an ice-cold stream, and the strong sulphur smell that pervades the atmosphere suggests unpleasant proximity to an Inferno. On our way to San Francisco we touched at Suva, the principal town in the Fiji Islands, and spent nearly a fortnight in the Hawaii Group, visiting Kilauea, the great volcano on Hawaii itself, and having a week or so in Honolulu, where the surf bathing is renowned. From San Francisco, which for practical purposes is a new city, dating from the great fire and earthquake of 1906, we went south by the old Spanish township of Monterey and Los Angeles to San Diego, a few miles from the Mexican frontier. From here, when the revolution was in progress in the latter country, daily "Come and see the War" motor excursions were run at five dollars a head. We broke the very tedious trans-continental railway journey at the Grand Canyon, Colorado. Nowhere has Dame Nature given a finer example of her prowess. The superb dignity and grandeur of the towering cliffs make a lasting impression; it is one of the wonders of the world. *Via* Chicago and Niagara Fall we proceeded to New York, and after encountering a storm—the proper article—in the Atlantic, we eventually put foot on dear old England again in the middle of last December. It will be seen that for thirteen months we were unceasingly "on the go." Novel sights and fresh objects of interest continuously confronted us, and it is only now that I am able to sort and classify the numberless ideas and impressions that have been tumbling over each other in their eagerness to imprint themselves on my brain. The joys of travel are great, the experiences are varied and often remarkable, but when all is said and done "there is no place like home" to live in.

J. E. R.

Arthur Hickman's letters from the front

17/12/14

Darling Mother, Father + all

I think it is about time I wrote for Xmas, and so I will wish you all a very very merry Xmas + happy New Year, and May we all be together again very soon after the New Year begins. I really don't know how long this will last, but I hope not too long, and if only the ones who had the Management of these things could only go + live

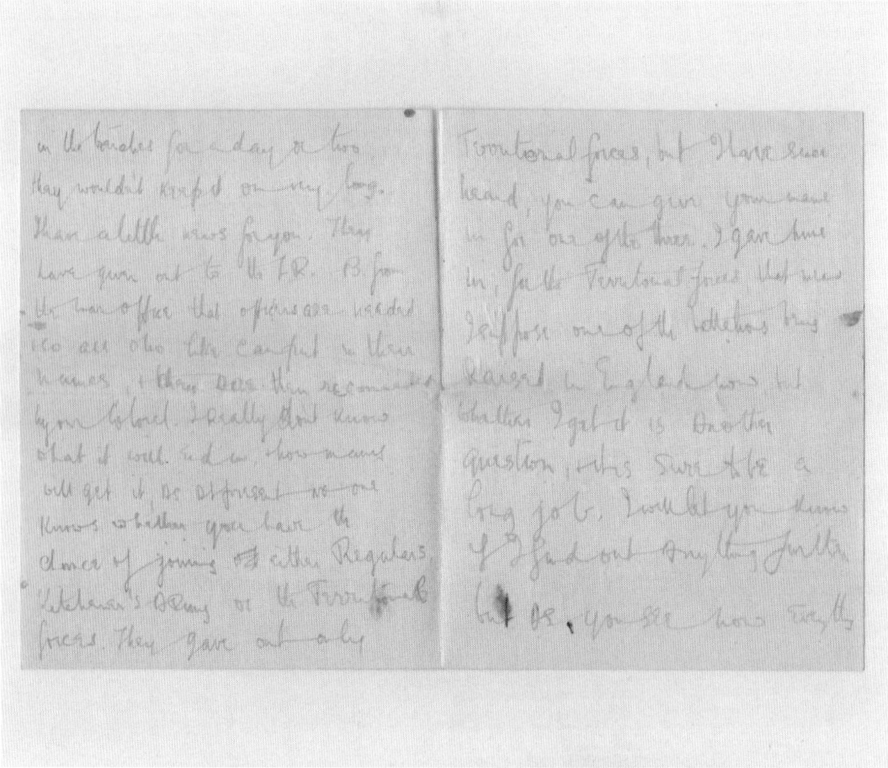

is uncertain & perhaps nothing may come of it. I am sorry I can't give anything in the way of presents, but I send my very best love & good wishes to you all & I do hope you will all be together again very soon. Thank you all so much for your Xmas parcels; I expect I will get them very soon now. My best love & good wishes to all

Love from

Arthur

A new view of The Oval

This photograph, which neither the author nor editor had seen before, shows a clear view into the ground, with military personnel present. The newspaper is dated August 8th 1914, just four days after war was declared. At this time "It'll be over by Christmas" was the belief of most. Little were they to know the carnage and colossal loss of life which was to follow. The photograph was found in a local library in a folder containing information about Surrey CCC.

Acknowledgements

A truly staggering number of people have helped me in the compilation of this book. How to acknowledge them all has caused me something of a headache. I have therefore listed each casualty on the war memorial about whom help was given and below their name indicated those who assisted me with school, social life and career details, or by sending me photographs. If a casualty is missing in this list it is because the work on them is all my own.

Charles Aldrich

John Wepsber for sending me the photograph of his grave. Cauis College, Cambridge for supplying me with details of his family and military career.

Ernest Attwater

David Underdown for sending me details about his social life, Alan Regan for supplying me the photograph of the memorial in Holy Trinity Church, Cuckfield and the photograph of his grave and Roger Packham for sending me a photograph of him.

Henry Blacklidge

Roger Packham for sending me a photograph of him.

William Burrell

Stephen Roberts for sending me a photograph of the war memorial on which he is listed and David Sawyer for sending me details of local churches in Northumberland.

Hubert Cattley

John Wepsber for sending me the photograph of his grave and Julian Reid at Merton College, Oxford for supplying me with details of his academic career.

Esme Chinnery

Mrs P Hatfield for sending me details of his schooldays and Roger Packham for sending me newspaper reports about his death.

Harry Chinnery

Roger Packham for sending me a copy of *Cricket* magazine dated July 28th 1904 and Mrs P Hatfield for sending details of his schooldays.

Wilfred Curwen

Iain Taylor for sending me a photograph of him, Norman Epps for supplying extra details about his sports career, the photograph of him in the Old Carthusians football team group and his Military Index Card, Pierre Vandervelden for sending me the photograph of the war memorial on which he is listed. Robin Darwall-Smith, Dr. David Roberts and Professor Richard Sheppard of "The Dusk Project" at Magdalen College Oxford have been hugely helpful in providing photographs and biographical details.

George Cooper

Christopher Jupp for sending me a photograph of him and for supplying military career details and Sebastian Cooper for sending me photographs of him.

William Gill

Soraya Cerio for sending me a photograph of him and providing details of his schooldays.

Francis Gillespie

Soraya Cerio for sending me a photograph of him and providing details of his schooldays.

Reginald Gipps

Chris Gare for allowing me to use photographs and other data from his website which covers the Gipps family and Jo Gosney for taking the photograph of the war memorial and allowing me to use it.

C Green

Bill Gordon for helping with access to old yearbooks and Iain Taylor for assisting with dates of membership for various Greens.

Arthur Hickman

Lucy Nash for sending me details about his schooldays and Charles Tilbury for photographs.

Charles Hoare

Graeme Clarke, Robert Goldwater and Bruce Hubbard for sending me details about his military career.

Bernard Holloway

Susan Webb at Jesus College, Cambridge and The Natives for sending me photographs of him.

John Howell

Paul Stevens and John Walker for sending me details of his schooldays, Paul Stevens on behalf of Repton School for sending me photographs of him from the school's records and Pierre Vandervelden for sending me the photograph of the war memorial on which he is listed.

Dudley Jewell

John Wepsber for sending me the photograph of his grave.

Albert Lane-Joynt

John Wepsber for sending me the photograph of his grave and Iain Taylor for sending me a copy of an article from the *Cricketer* and Clare Sargent for sending me a photograph of him.

Richard Lewis

Iain Taylor for sending me a photograph of him taken from *Famous Cricketers and Cricket Grounds* by Charles Alcock. Robin Darwall-Smith for sending me details of his academic career.

Edward Longton

Elizabeth Wells for sending me details about his schooldays.

Alan Marshal

Jo Miller for sending me a photograph of him and Andrew Renshaw for sending me a photograph of his grave.

Harold May

Rachel Hassall on behalf of Sherborne School for sending me a photograph of him in a school cricket team and Janet Dean for sending me details of his schooldays.

Edwin Myers

John Wepsber for sending me the photograph of his grave, Naomi Klein for informing me about the war memorial that he is listed on and Paul Harrison and Ed Miller for sending me details of his Army and football careers and a photograph of him in the Northfleet football team group.

John Nason

Mike Spurrier for sending me a photograph of him.

Frank Nightingale

Soraya Cerio for sending me a photograph of him and providing details of his schooldays.

Harold Noakes

Naomi Klein for telling me about the two war memorials in churches that he is listed on in Clapham. Sally Gilbert and the Merchant Taylor's School Archive for permission to use the photograph of the school's war memorial.

Erasmus Parker

Anne Turner for sending me details of his military career and Pierre Vandervelden for sending me the photograph of his grave.

Howard Parkes

Roger Packham for sending me details about his funeral.

John Raphael

Roy Hough for sending me a selection of photographs of him. Sally Gilbert and the Merchant Taylor's School Archive for permission to use the photograph of the school's war memorial and pages from the book that he wrote.

Arthur Beddome Read

Charles Woollam for sending me a picture of his memorial.

Wilfred Francis Reay

John Wepsber for sending me a picture of the Thiepval Mermorial.

Francis Robarts

William Wood for taking me to see the school war memorial at The Whitgift School on which he is listed and then sending me a photograph of it and giving permission to use the photograph.

Elvin Scott

Graeme Clarke for supplying details about his award of the Military Cross.

Victor Shrapnel

Nathan Cole and Chris Burton regarding photographs and his schooldays, Russ Towes for details about his life and military career and Norman Epps for telling me that Wilson's Grammar School played cricket at The Oval. Robin Darwall-Smith, Dr. David Roberts and Professor Richard Sheppard of "The Dusk Project" at Magdalen College, Oxford have provided photographs and biographical details.

Charles Sills

John Wepsber for sending me the photograph of the memorial on which he is listed.

Christopher Snell

Clifford Davies and Pamela Taylor for sending me details about his schooldays.

Arthur Thorne

David Bird for taking the time to visit the churchyard and photograph his grave and allowing me to use it in this book.

Carleton Tufnell

Roger Packham for sending me a photograph of him.

Walter Whittle

John Wepsber for sending me a photograph of his grave and Soraya Cerio for sending me a photograph of him and providing details of his schooldays.

Guy Wormald

Mrs P Hatfield for sending details of this schooldays, Joe Eastwood for sending me details about his military career and Richard King for finding a photograph of him.

Philip Wynter

Pierre Vandervelden for sending me the photograph of his grave.